GOALS AND OBJECTIVES FOR DEVELOPING NORMAL MOVEMENT PATTERNS

A Manual of Gross Motor Behavior Objectives with an Emphasis on the Quality of Movement

Julie Zimmerman, RPT
(NDT Certified)

AN ASPEN PUBLICATION®
Aspen Publishers, Inc.
Gaithersburg, Maryland
1988

Library of Congress Cataloging-in-Publication Data

Zimmerman, Julie
Goals and objectives for developing normal movement patterns.

Includes index.
1. Movement disorders in children—Patients—Rehabilitation.
2. Physical therapy for children. I. Title.
RJ496.M68Z56 1988 618.92'74062 87-35125
ISBN: 0-87189-758-X

Editorial Services: Marsha Davies

Library of Congress Catalog Card Number: 87-35125
ISBN: 0-87189-758-X

Printed in the United States of America

3 4 5

To Sandy

I would like to gratefully acknowledge the
assistance of Paula Spyropulos, OTR,
and Sharon McAllister, OTR, who
freely gave their expertise
and support.

Contents

Introduction

This manual starts with the premise that it is impossible to accurately describe a student's occupational or physical therapy program by means of a list of behavioral objectives. A therapeutic approach involves a constant process of re-evaluation, and techniques, activities, and objectives should change to reflect the student's changing response to the therapist's input. Further, the development of motor skills rarely follows a predictable timetable.

Nevertheless, therapists are expected to develop clear, measurable treatment goals for the student to accomplish within a specific time. It is difficult to satisfy this requirement because statements that are broad enough to give an accurate overview of a treatment program are the most difficult to measure. As an example of the problem, the goal of improving proximal stability is broad, hard to measure, is unclear to nontherapists, and, unlike the student, doesn't change year to year. On the other hand, a statement such as "The student will imitate a 3-step unilateral upper body motor pattern with a verbal cue 2 out of 4 times" is so specific it reflects only a minute part of the therapy program. To complicate the task, most resources intended to help therapists develop educational plans concentrate on gross motor milestones and isolated muscle actions.

Developmentally disabled children cannot successfully be approached in terms of static milestones and measurements. First, severely handicapped children may make important gains and never move up on a milestone chart. A child who never develops head control may achieve the goal of reduced dominance of hyperextension tone, which would significantly affect the ease of positioning, feeding, dressing, transfers, etc.

Opportunities for learning and fun are multiplied for a child who can sit comfortably and swallow easily, even though scoring 0 on a milestone chart.

Second, how a child moves can be as important as what skills are present. In the absence of normal movement components, developmentally disabled children compensate by using abnormal tone and movement patterns in order to achieve their motor goals. Such "milestones" are hardly a true indication of function. They are energy consuming (leaving little endurance or concentration for other activities), are abnormal in appearance (interfering with peer interaction and the development of a positive self-image), and are unable to provide effective stability and mobility at the same time. Motor skills based on abnormal patterns are also self-limiting. The more difficult an activity, the more compensation required, which reinforces abnormal tone, strengthening the very components which make normal movement impossible. If therapists do not look at the progression of dysfunction, address the abnormalities and imbalances, and develop the missing movement components, they help preserve abnormal movement and ultimately limit function.

This manual includes gross motor goals and objectives for improving the quality of movement. The objectives describe the opportunities for progress available to severely handicapped students. Motor goals are broken down extensively and sequenced to show the movement components necessary to reach them. The achievement of qualitative milestones is the prerequisite for optimum educational success in the classroom and on the playground and it influences all areas of development. Compromises are inevitable because of each child's deformities, home environment, medical complications, and behavior and because of limitations of space, time, and equipment. But whatever the handicap and the preferred treatment approach, maximizing quality of movement maximizes function.

How To Use This Book

Regulations for educational plans specify that objectives must consist of three parts: (1) a behavior, (2) a condition, and (3) a measurement. They must be stated in terms of what a student should achieve rather than in terms of the therapist's input.

This manual is divided into eight sections (I, II, III, etc.) corresponding to eight major areas that affect gross motor development (tone, righting and equilibrium, etc.). In each section there is a table for each therapeutic goal. For example, in the section on tone, the first table is for the goal Reduction of Hypertension Tonus and the second is for Reduction of Primitive Reflexes. Each table lists (1) behaviors for reaching the goal (1, 2, 3, . . .), (2) conditions (A, B, C, . . .), and (3) measurements (a, b, c, . . .). In the table for Reduction of Hypertension Tonus, the column of behaviors begins with the words "The student will" and continues with a list of behaviors, the first item of which is "relax when passively positioned in flexion." The second column contains a list of conditions and the third a list of measurements. In constructing objectives to aid in reaching the goal, choose items from each column. For example, one objective might be the following:

> The student will demonstrate body righting on body in supine (behavior) with facilitation (condition) in 0–5 seconds (measurement) [II-10 E f].

Objectives can be constructed that are even narrower by choosing more than one item from the measurements column, as in the following example:

The student will creep backward reciprocally in quadruped (behavior) with tactile cues (condition) for 20 feet (measurement) in 30–60 seconds (measurement) 2 out of 4 times (measurement) [IV-13 F t h b].

At the end of every section, there is a table with a blank behaviors column; this allows therapists to add behaviors that are not already listed if they so desire. The lists of conditions and measurements are the same in all tables; they are printed in each table for convenience.

Some behaviors are listed in the index as being in several sections. The choice of which section to refer to depends on the student's deficit and the goal being addressed in therapy.

Example 1. If a student toe walks, the objective chosen for addressing the problem will depend on the cause of the toe walking. The approach may be to reduce hypertonus (if there is spasticity of plantar flexors), to increase postural tone (if the student uses hyperextension to compensate for hypotonus), or to improve the gait pattern (if toe walking is a poor gait habit).

Example 2. "The student will assume standing through half-kneeling." This behavior is indexed under Proximal Stability (III) and under Locomotion and Gait (IV). The choice of objective depends on the desired emphasis. For instance, are you working on the trunk stability that allows the dissociation necessary to perform the activity or are you teaching independence in gait?

Example 3. If a student can't walk, assisted ambulation around the playground for practice is probably not the most effective approach. Why can't the student walk? Does he or she have the pelvic stability necessary for standing, weight shifting, and gait? What components are missing for a normal gait pattern? Working on equilibrium in sitting may well be the quickest way to ambulation for some students.

Example 4. If a specific developmental skill is weak, is that reason enough to work on it in therapy? There may be different reasons to incorporate it into a therapy program. Or it may be decided that time is better spent working on other skills. For example, the skill of rolling could be added to a program for a variety of reasons:

- rolling to inhibit hyperextension tone (II-22 or II-28)
- rolling to reinforce righting reactions and prepare for equilibrium (II-31 or II-42)
- rolling to develop independent locomotion (IV-2 or IV-3)
- rolling for speed and control to allow participation in physical education class (VII-45 or VII-48)

Determining why a specific skill should be addressed in therapy helps make it a therapeutic exercise, not just a gross motor activity.

Example 5. A possible sequence of objectives to reach the goal of independent sitting follows:

1. The student will increase range at shoulders and hips to assume a full prone position with arms overhead with facilitation for 30–60 seconds (VI-29 E h).
2. The student will demonstrate an amphibian reaction with facilitation 4 out of 4 times (II-36 E d).
3. The student will increase abdominal strength with moderate to minimum assistance to functional level (I-77 B v).
4. The student will maintain weight on hands in prone positions with proprioceptive cues for 5–30 seconds (III-17 G g).
5. The student will maintain upper extremities in proper alignment in weightbearing with verbal cue 3 out of 4 times (III-23 I c).

6. The student will right head and body against gravity to come to sitting with tactile cue for 2–5 repetitions (II-41 F l).
7. The student will assume and maintain sidesitting on the nonpreferred side with facilitation for 5–30 seconds (III-193 E g).
8 The student will maintain the pelvis in neutral in sitting independently 90% of the time (III-201 K e).
9. The student will bring head, shoulders, and trunk into alignment over the base of support in sitting with verbal cue for 2–5 repetitions (III-204 I l).

Without the righting and proximal stability developed by these types of activities, the achievement of aligned, stable sitting is unlikely.

It is important for therapists to think in terms of the deficits which cause an inability to perform skills and of the appropriate treatment to redress them. If therapists are quality-oriented, they are less apt to lay scatter skills on an unstable base and more apt to give children the prerequisites for functional mobility.

Conditions and Measurements

Conditions reflect how much help a student needs to accomplish a behavior and *measurements* reflect to what extent the behavior is performed. Conditions and measurements determine the functional significance of an objective, such as in the following examples:

- The student will perform transfers between a wheelchair and toilet independently in 5 minutes.
- The student will perform transfers between a wheelchair and toilet with guarding assistance 3 out of 4 times.
- The student will perform transfers between a wheelchair and toilet with maximum assistance in 20 minutes.

These objectives refer to students with vastly different needs relative to inservice and consult time, teacher involvement, scheduling, and therapy goals.

A long-term goal may incorporate a sequence of objectives where the behavior stays the same while the conditions or measurements change, as shown below:

1. The student will use an upper extremity prosthesis as an assist with moderate to minimum assistance 100% of the time.
2. The student will use an upper extremity prosthesis as an assist with tactile cues 50% of the time.

3. The student will use an upper extremity prosthesis as an assist with tactile cues 100% of the time.
4. The student will use an upper extremity prosthesis as an assist with verbal cue 100% of the time.
5. The student will use an upper extremity prosthesis as an assist in the therapy setting 50% of the time.
6. The student will use an upper extremity prosthesis as an assist in the therapy setting 100% of the time.
7. The student will use an upper extremity prosthesis as an assist in functional activities 50% of the time.
8. The student will use an upper extremity prosthesis as an assist in functional activities 100% of the time.

Since terminology differs among therapists, definitions of the conditions referred to in this manual follow:

● With *maximum to moderate assistance*, the student helps to perform an activity, but the therapist does more of the work. For example:

—The therapist puts on a lower extremity brace and fastens the lower strap; the student fastens the upper straps.
—To regain a sitting position in the wheelchair, the student reaches back for the armrest while the therapist lifts the pelvis into the chair.

● With *moderate to minimum assistance*, the student does the majority of the task. For example:

—The student hops with only the hands held for support.
—The student walks with a rollator but help in steering it is provided.

- By filling in the blank in *with __% assistance*, the therapist can indicate more specifically, though somewhat arbitrarily, the amount of help needed: perhaps 100% (student put through activity passively), 75% (maximum assistance), 50% (moderate assistance), or 25% (minimum assistance).
- With *guarding assistance*, the student performs the activity independently but with questionable safety so that someone must be present and ready to provide support.
- Understanding the concept of *facilitation* is vital for promoting normal movement. Facilitation requires much more than mere assistance and is to be understood here as it is with a neurodevelopmental treatment (NDT) orientation. NDT is a quality-concerned approach to treating developmental disabilities, where a child is handled in such a way as to improve postural tone and elicit active movement in normal alignment. Facilitation is handling with a precise use of tactile, proprioceptive, positional, and directional cues to stimulate the child's own nervous system to produce the desired response. The purpose is to achieve proper body alignment and preparation of the neuromuscular system so that when the child moves, he or she experiences the sensory motor feedback of normal movement. This is necessary for motor learning to occur. The amount of facilitation given is based on feedback received from the child and decreases as the child begins to be able to control tone, symmetry, and alignment. Facilitation, like assistance, is kept to the minimum necessary to maintain quality while maximizing independence and functional level. Consider this example. *Assisting* an equilibrium response in standing could involve holding a child's hands for support while weight shifting with a tilt board (moderate to minimum assistance) or holding and guiding the child's trunk (maximum to moderate assistance). To *facilitate* an equilibrium response in standing (weight shift

9

to right), the therapist's hands might be placed on the child's right gluteals and hip (right hand) and left abdominals (left hand) to give the following cues: (1) a proprioceptive cue to right hip with (2) a tactile and (3) a directional cue to the right gluteals to posteriorly tilt the pelvis on the weightbearing side for stability; (4) a tactile cue to the left abdominals with a (5) flexion and (6) rotational cue on the nonweightbearing side; meanwhile both hands (7) shift the weight to the right and (8) control the speed of response. With this hand placement the therapist is providing cues to prepare appropriate musculature and control alignment, direction, and speed. The child is actively producing trunk elongation on the right and the lower extremity components of equilibrium and has actively experienced and reinforced the normal response to a weight shift. The preceding description may sound complicated, confusing, or intimidating, but remember that therapists both facilitate and inhibit muscles *every time they touch a student.* Choosing where and how your hands are placed maximizes the input to the appropriate alpha motor neurons and the chances for a successful motor response.

- Examples of *tactile cues* are (1) facilitatory input to a muscle (tapping the quadriceps prior to active knee extension) and (2) a directional touch (tapping the arm forward as a reminder of proper alignment in weightbearing).
- An example of a *proprioceptive cue* is joint compression (compression at the shoulder toward the palm in all fours) to facilitate upper extremity weightbearing.
- A *demonstration* provides the child with a visual model so he or she can either receive visual cues throughout an activity or first watch and then imitate the movements.
- *Verbal cues* can range from complete instructions during an activity to brief reminders before it begins or when the student gets stuck.
- The following (and last) three conditions entail that the student carries out an activity without help. However, skills performed in the controlled environment of a familiar

therapy room at a certain time of day or after sequenced preparation may disappear outside of therapy. These skills then fulfill objectives *in the therapy setting. Performing skills independently* entails that the skills can be done in a variety of settings. *In functional activities*, the student not only can perform the skills but remembers to do so outside of the range of adult supervision.

Therapists are encouraged to make their own additions to the lists of conditions and measurements that occur in the tables for the various goals in each section below.

Table of Goals

Tone   I

Tone is difficult to define, treat, and measure, let alone explain to a parent or teacher. Therapists use the terms *muscle tone, postural tone, hyperextension tone, hypertonus, hypotonus, spastic tone, flexor tone, normal tone,* and *abnormal tone.* Clinical measurement of changes in tone is an imprecise science and is most often done by looking at changes in postures, functional skills, endurance, etc.

The NDT approach to normal development provides an understanding for treating abnormal tone. In normal development a baby is born with strong flexor tone (physiological flexion), which disappears during the first one to two months. Extension, the first antigravity movement, begins to build at two to three months from prone, with antigravity flexion appearing around four months from supine. After the balance of flexion and extension is achieved, antigravity lateral flexion develops from sidelying. The balance of antigravity flexor and extensor tone allows the body to stabilize against gravity as well as move in proper alignment. With developmental disabilities the flexion components don't develop sufficiently to balance extension, so a baby will compensate with prolonged primitive and poor quality movements, which develop into abnormal movement patterns. To stabilize against gravity, the baby compensates by "fixing" (using his or her extension to stiffen the body), thereby preventing further movement of that segment and interfering with the normal process of increasing mobility and stability together. The lack of stability with mobility will interfere with all aspects of development (rotation, weight shifts, righting, equilibrium, dissociation, range of motion, hand use, manipulation, gaze, convergence, and body image).

Primitive reflexes are tone building tools in the normal child. Just as a CP child gets stuck with an imbalance of extension over flexion, so that child may also not develop the control to overcome the dominance of the early reflexes and may reinforce them by learning to use them for movement or stability.

The objectives in this manual are based on the following definitions of tone.

Muscle tone is the readiness of a muscle to contract, its resistance to stretch, or its resting tension. *Hypertonus* or *hypotonus* is usually evaluated in individual muscles or muscle groups by a quick stretch to elicit the stretch reflex.

Spastic tone, hyperextension tone, abnormal tone are used interchangeably to describe the abnormal hypertonus which develops when antigravity extension is not modified by the development of more advanced movement. It can result in fixing (stiffening with decreased range of motion) or flailing (bursts of uncontrolled movement). Although a developmentally disabled child uses hyperextension tone for stability and mobility (though not at the same time), it is poorly controlled, inefficient movement and often can only be used in whole body stereotyped patterns. Children evaluated as hypertonic commonly have hypotonic proximal tone at rest and high tone in the limbs, which is the opposite of normal tone distribution.

Flexor tone develops with controlled antigravity flexion and balances normal extensor tone. Flexor tone should not be confused with the position of flexion. If the child with abnormal tone is frequently placed in sitting, he may fall into a fully flexed position to avoid going over backwards and over time may develop deformities of flexion. The excessive flexion in this case is the result of gravity versus excessive strength of flexors. Likewise spastic flexion patterns of the limbs develop originally because of abnormal alignment caused by the early tone imbalance. A child in a position of excessive flexion frequently has poor flexor tone.

Postural tone is a balance of controlled antigravity flexor and extensor tone and is absolutely essential for normal movement. Without it one can stabilize the body, but one needs to use so much hypertonus that the rigidity will limit turning the head or using the limbs, as with spasticity. One can have an excess of mobility with precarious control and balance, as with athetosis. In order to develop postural tone in the developmentally disabled child, the therapist must first inhibit the primitive and abnormal patterns and tone that are used for compensatory movement and may dominate movement, and then build flexor tone. Establishing better postural tone gives the child the base for moving on to effective righting and equilibrium reactions and proximal stability.

Hypertonus or hypotonus affects oral musculature as well as other voluntary muscles. This section ends with objectives concerning oral-motor tone, movement, stability, and feeding.

Reduction of Hypertension Tonus

Behaviors	Conditions	Measurements
The student will 1. relax when passively positioned in flexion 2. relax for body to be positioned out of hyperextension in sidelying 3. relax for body to be positioned out of hyperextension in prone 4. relax for body to be positioned out of hyperextension in supine 5. relax sufficiently to allow supported sitting 6. tolerate patterns of dissociation with passive positioning 7. inhibit head thrust into extension in supported sitting 8. inhibit flailing of limbs with voluntary relaxation 9. inhibit hyperextension with voluntary relaxation 10. actively flex 1 body part to break up hyperextension posturing 11. maintain a position of reduced hyperextension 12. maintain patterns of dissociation with passive positioning	A. with maximum–moderate assistance B. with moderate–minimum assistance C. with __% assistance D. with guarding assistance E. with facilitation F. with tactile cues G. with proprioceptive cues H. with a demonstration I. with verbal cues J. in the therapy setting K. independently L. in functional activities	a. 1 out of 4 times b. 2 out of 4 times c. 3 out of 4 times d. 4 out of 4 times e. __% of the time f in/for 0–5 seconds g. in/for 5–30 seconds h. in/for 30–60 seconds i. in/for over 1 minute j. in/for __ minutes k. 1 repetition l. 2–5 repetitions m. 6–10 repetitions n. over 10 repetitions o. __ repetitions p. 0–5 feet q. 5–15 feet r. 15–25 feet s. over 25 feet t. __ feet u. to/at mid range/level v. to/at functional range/level w. to/at normal limits x. to/at __% of normal y. to/at __ degrees

Reduction of Hypertension Tonus continued

Behaviors	Conditions	Measurements
13. maintain the upper extremities in a position of reduced hypertonic posturing 14. maintain the lower extremities in a position of reduced hypertonic posturing 15. maintain relaxation with a change of position 16. maintain relaxation in supported sitting 17. maintain relaxation while being carried or transferred 18. inhibit flailing while being pushed in wheelchair 19. maintain relaxation while being pushed in wheelchair 20. maintain relaxation while being positioned in wheelchair 21. maintain relaxation while being positioned in adaptive equipment 22. maintain relaxation while being diapered 23. maintain relaxation while being toiletted 24. maintain relaxation while being dressed 25. maintain relaxation during washing and grooming	A. with maximum– moderate assistance B. with moderate– minimum assistance C. with __% assistance D. with guarding assistance E. with facilitation F. with tactile cues G. with proprioceptive cues H. with a demonstration I. with verbal cues J. in the therapy setting K. independently L. in functional activities	a. 1 out of 4 times b. 2 out of 4 times c. 3 out of 4 times d. 4 out of 4 times e. __% of the time f. in/for 0–5 seconds g. in/for 5–30 seconds h. in/for 30–60 seconds i. in/for over 1 minute j. in/for __ minutes k. 1 repetition l. 2–5 repetitions m. 6–10 repetitions n. over 10 repetitions o. __ repetitions p. 0–5 feet q. 5–15 feet r. 15–25 feet s. over 25 feet t. __ feet u. to/at mid range/level v. to/at functional range/level w. to/at normal limits x. to/at __% of normal y. to/at __ degrees

Reduction of Hypertension Tonus continued

Behaviors	Conditions	Measurements
26. maintain relaxation while being bathed 27. inhibit flailing while being assisted in ADL 28. maintain relaxation while being assisted in ADL	A. with maximum–moderate assistance B. with moderate–minimum assistance C. with __% assistance D. with guarding assistance E. with facilitation F. with tactile cues G. with proprioceptive cues H. with a demonstration I. with verbal cues J. in the therapy setting K. independently L. in functional activities	a. 1 out of 4 times b. 2 out of 4 times c. 3 out of 4 times d. 4 out of 4 times e. __% of the time f. in/for 0–5 seconds g. in/for 5–30 seconds h. in/for 30–60 seconds i. in/for over 1 minute j. in/for __ minutes k. 1 repetition l. 2–5 repetitions m. 6–10 repetitions n. over 10 repetitions o. __ repetitions p. 0–5 feet q. 5–15 feet r. 15–25 feet s. over 25 feet t. __ feet u. to/at mid range/level v. to/at functional range/level w. to/at normal limits x. to/at __% of normal y. to/at __ degrees

Reduction of Dominance of Primitive Reflexes

Behaviors	Conditions	Measurements
The student will		
29. maintain extended position of leg upon stimulation to sole of foot (flexor withdrawal)	A. with maximum–moderate assistance	a. 1 out of 4 times
	B. with moderate–minimum assistance	b. 2 out of 4 times
30. maintain position of leg upon stimulation to medial surface of opposite leg (crossed extension)	C. with _% assistance	c. 3 out of 4 times
	D. with guarding assistance	d. 4 out of 4 times
31. maintain flexion of leg upon passive flexion of opposite leg (crossed extension)	E. with facilitation	e. _% of the time
	F. with tactile cues	f. in/for 0–5 seconds
32. inhibit excessive startle reaction (Moro)	G. with proprioceptive cues	g. in/for 5–30 seconds
33. relax excessive flexion of legs in supported standing	H. with a demonstration	h. in/for 30–60 seconds
	I. with verbal cues	i. in/for over 1 minute
34. allow passive flexion of limbs in supine (STLR)	J. in the therapy setting	j. in/for _ minutes
	K. independently	k. 1 repetition
35. relax to inhibit flexion in prone (STLR)	L. in functional activities	l. 2–5 repetitions
36. inhibit associated reaction of limb with active movement of opposite limb		m. 6–10 repetitions
		n. over 10 repetitions
37. relax excessive extensor tone of legs in supported standing		o. _ repetitions
		p. 0–5 feet
38. actively dissociate legs in supported standing		q. 5–15 feet
		r. 15–25 feet
39. relax excessive extension of spine and legs when thorax is held prone in space (Landau)		s. over 25 feet
		t. _ feet
		u. to/at mid range/level
		v. to/at functional range/level
		w. to/at normal limits
		x. to/at _% of normal
		y. to/at _ degrees

Reduction of Dominance of Tonic Neck Reflexes

Behaviors	Conditions	Measurements
The student will 40. maintain position and tone of limbs with left-right head movements (ATNR) 41. maintain weightbearing position of limbs with left-right head movements (ATNR) 42. maintain position and tone of limbs with up-down head movements (STNR) 43. maintain weightbearing position of limbs with up-down head movements (STNR) 44. dissociate head from body movements	A. with maximum–moderate assistance B. with moderate–minimum assistance C. with __% assistance D. with guarding assistance E. with facilitation F. with tactile cues G. with proprioceptive cues H. with a demonstration I. with verbal cues J. in the therapy setting K. independently L. in functional activities	a. 1 out of 4 times b. 2 out of 4 times c. 3 out of 4 times d. 4 out of 4 times e. __% of the time f. in/for 0–5 seconds g. in/for 5–30 seconds h. in/for 30–60 seconds i. in/for over 1 minute j. in/for __ minutes k. 1 repetition l. 2–5 repetitions m. 6–10 repetitions n. over 10 repetitions o. __ repetitions p. 0–5 feet q. 5–15 feet r. 15–25 feet s. over 25 feet t. __ feet u. to/at mid range/level v. to/at functional range/level w. to/at normal limits x. to/at __% of normal y. to/at __ degrees

Improvement of Flexion

Behaviors	Conditions	Measurements
The student will		
45. perform active flexion without hyperextension of other body parts	A. with maximum–moderate assistance	a. 1 out of 4 times
46. perform active flexion in prone positions	B. with moderate–minimum assistance	b. 2 out of 4 times
47. bring the head to midline in supine	C. with ___% assistance	c. 3 out of 4 times
48. maintain the head in midline in supine	D. with guarding assistance	d. 4 out of 4 times
49. lift head off surface in supine	E. with facilitation	e. ___% of the time
50. decrease head lag in pull to sit	F. with tactile cues	f. in/for 0–5 seconds
51. tuck chin in pull to sit	G. with proprioceptive cues	g. in/for 5–30 seconds
52. assume and maintain chin tuck	H. with a demonstration	h. in/for 30–60 seconds
53. raise arm in supine	I. with verbal cues	i. in/for over 1 minute
54. look at hand in supine	J. in the therapy setting	j. in/for ___ minutes
55. bring hand to mouth in supine	K. independently	k. 1 repetition
56. raise both arms in supine	L. in functional activities	l. 2–5 repetitions
57. bring hands together in supine		m. 6–10 repetitions
58. bring hands together in sidelying		n. over 10 repetitions
59. raise leg in supine		o. ___ repetitions
60. bring hands to foot in supine		p. 0–5 feet
61. raise both legs in supine		q. 5–15 feet
62. bring hands to feet in supine		r. 15–25 feet
63. bring foot to mouth in supine		s. over 25 feet
		t. ___ feet
		u. to/at mid range/level
		v. to/at functional range/level
		w. to/at normal limits
		x. to/at ___% of normal
		y. to/at ___ degrees

Improvement of Flexion continued

Behaviors	Conditions	Measurements
64. pull to sit	A. with maximum–moderate assistance	a. 1 out of 4 times
65. bring head forward in sitting	B. with moderate–minimum assistance	b. 2 out of 4 times
66. bring arms forward in sitting	C. with __% assistance	c. 3 out of 4 times
67. bring arms to midline in sitting	D. with guarding assistance	d. 4 out of 4 times
68. cross midline with arms in sitting	E. with facilitation	e. __% of the time
69. bring head/trunk forward to help in dressing	F. with tactile cues	f. in/for 0–5 seconds
70. raise arm(s) to help in dressing	G. with proprioceptive cues	g. in/for 5–30 seconds
71. raise leg(s) to help in dressing	H. with a demonstration	h. in/for 00–00 seconds
72. bring hands together to help in dressing	I. with verbal cues	i. in/for over 1 minute
73. relax lumbar lordosis	J. in the therapy setting	j. in/for __ minutes
74. maintain a posterior pelvic tilt	K. independently	k. 1 repetition
75. keep weight forward when tipped back in sitting	L. in functional activities	l. 2–5 repetitions
76. perform a sit-up		m. 6–10 repetitions
77. increase abdominal strength		n. over 10 repetitions
78. assume the supine flexion position		o. __ repetitions
79. maintain supine flexion		p. 0–5 feet
80. bring the feet overhead in supine with chin tucked		q. 5–15 feet
81. flex elbows while hanging on a flexion bar		r. 15–25 feet
		s. over 25 feet
		t. __ feet
		u. to/at mid range/level
		v. to/at functional range/level
		w. to/at normal limits
		x. to/at __% of normal
		y. to/at __ degrees

Improvement of Flexion continued

Behaviors	Conditions	Measurements
82. flex hips and knees while hanging on a flexion bar 83. flex elbows, hips, and knees while hanging on a flexion bar	A. with maximum–moderate assistance B. with moderate–minimum assistance C. with __% assistance D. with guarding assistance E. with facilitation F. with tactile cues G. with proprioceptive cues H. with a demonstration I. with verbal cues J. in the therapy setting K. independently L. in functional activities	a. 1 out of 4 times b. 2 out of 4 times c. 3 out of 4 times d. 4 out of 4 times e. __% of the time f. in/for 0–5 seconds g. in/for 5–30 seconds h. in/for 30–60 seconds i. in/for over 1 minute j. in/for __ minutes k. 1 repetition l. 2–5 repetitions m. 6–10 repetitions n. over 10 repetitions o. __ repetitions p. 0–5 feet q. 5–15 feet r. 15–25 feet s. over 25 feet t. __ feet u. to/at mid range/level v. to/at functional range/level w. to/at normal limits x. to/at __% of normal y. to/at __ degrees

Increased Postural Tone without Increased Hyperextension Tonus

Behaviors	Conditions	Measurements
The student will	A. with maximum–moderate assistance	a. 1 out of 4 times
84. perform bridging in supine without back extensor spasm	B. with moderate–minimum assistance	b. 2 out of 4 times
85. perform bridging in supine with neck in flexion	C. with __% assistance	c. 3 out of 4 times
86. perform bridging to assist in dressing	D. with guarding assistance	d. 4 out of 4 times
87. lift the head into extension in prone positions without hypertonic posturing of limbs	E. with facilitation	e. __% of the time
88. maintain head in extension in prone without hypertonic posturing of limbs	F. with tactile cues	f. in/for 0–5 seconds
89. maintain head in midline with neck extension in prone	G. with proprioceptive cues	g. in/for 5–30 seconds
90. extend the neck and trunk in prone positions without hypertonic posturing of limbs	H. with a demonstration	h. in/for 30–60 seconds
91. extend the legs in prone positions without hypertonic posturing of arms	I. with verbal cues	i. in/for over 1 minute
92. extend the wrist and fingers for upper extremity weightbearing	J. in the therapy setting	j. in/for __ minutes
93. relax the foot and ankle for lower extremity weightbearing	K. independently	k. 1 repetition
	L. in functional activities	l. 2–5 repetitions
		m. 6–10 repetitions
		n. over 10 repetitions
		o. __ repetitions
		p. 0–5 feet
		q. 5–15 feet
		r. 15–25 feet
		s. over 25 feet
		t. __ feet
		u. to/at mid range/level
		v. to/at functional range/level
		w. to/at normal limits
		x. to/at __% of normal
		y. to/at __ degrees

Increased Postural Tone without Increased Hyperextension Tonus continued

Behaviors	Conditions	Measurements
94. bring the head to neutral in supported sitting	A. with maximum– moderate assistance	a. 1 out of 4 times
	B. with moderate– minimum assistance	b. 2 out of 4 times
95. maintain the head in neutral in supported sitting		c. 3 out of 4 times
	C. with __% assistance	d. 4 out of 4 times
96. bring the head to neutral in antigravity positions	D. with guarding assistance	e. __% of the time
		f. in/for 0–5 seconds
	E. with facilitation	g. in/for 5–30 seconds
97. maintain the head in neutral in antigravity positions	F. with tactile cues	h. in/for 30–60 seconds
	G. with proprioceptive cues	i. in/for over 1 minute
98. maintain the head in neutral with neck rotations		j. in/for __ minutes
	H. with a demonstration	k. 1 repetition
	I. with verbal cues	l. 2–5 repetitions
99. maintain the head in neutral with movements of the limbs	J. in the therapy setting	m. 6–10 repetitions
	K. independently	n. over 10 repetitions
100. maintain the head in neutral with movements of the trunk	L. in functional activities	o. __ repetitions
		p. 0–5 feet
		q. 5–15 feet
101. maintain the head in neutral during active movement transitions		r. 15–25 feet
		s. over 25 feet
		t. __ feet
102. maintain an upright position against gravity with pelvic support		u. to/at mid range/level
		v. to/at functional range/level
103. maintain an upright position against gravity with trunk in neutral and arms relaxed with pelvic support		w. to/at normal limits
		x. to/at __% of normal
		y. to/at __ degrees

Increased Postural Tone without Increased Hyperextension Tonus continued

Behaviors	Conditions	Measurements
104. maintain an upright position against gravity	A. with maximum–moderate assistance	a. 1 out of 4 times
105. maintain an upright position against gravity with trunk in neutral and arms relaxed	B. with moderate–minimum assistance	b. 2 out of 4 times
	C. with __% assistance	c. 3 out of 4 times
	D. with guarding assistance	d. 4 out of 4 times
106. maintain an upright position against gravity with pelvis in neutral	E. with facilitation	e. __% of the time
	F. with tactile cues	f. in/for 0–5 seconds
107. maintain an upright posture without increased hypertonus	G. with proprioceptive cues	g. in/for 5–30 seconds
	H. with a demonstration	h. in/for 30–60 seconds
108. maintain reduced tonus in an upright posture with movement of arms	I. with verbal cues	i. in/for over 1 minute
	J. in the therapy setting	j. in/for __ minutes
109. maintain reduced tonus in an upright posture with neck and trunk rotation	K. independently	k. 1 repetition
	L. in functional activities	l. 2–5 repetitions
110. maintain reduced tonus in an upright posture with weight shifts		m. 6–10 repetitions
		n. over 10 repetitions
111. maintain reduced tonus in an upright posture for ADL		o. __ repetitions
		p. 0–5 feet
112. maintain reduced tonus in an upright posture for fine motor activities		q. 5–15 feet
		r. 15–25 feet
113. maintain reduced tonus during active movement transitions		s. over 25 feet
		t. __ feet
		u. to/at mid range/level
		v. to/at functional range/level
		w. to/at normal limits
		x. to/at __% of normal
		y. to/at __ degrees

Normalization of Tone To Permit Oral Motor Functions

Behaviors	Conditions	Measurements
The student will	A. with maximum–moderate assistance	a. 1 out of 4 times
114. assume stable, aligned posture in preparation for oral motor activities	B. with moderate–minimum assistance	b. 2 out of 4 times
115. maintain head in neutral for oral motor activities	C. with —% assistance	c. 3 out of 4 times
116. reduce dominance of tonic bite	D. with guarding assistance	d. 4 out of 4 times
117. reduce dominance of rooting reflex	E. with facilitation	e. —% of the time
118. reduce dominance of sucking reflex	F. with tactile cues	f. in/for 0–5 seconds
119. inhibit tongue thrust	G. with proprioceptive cues	g. in/for 5–30 seconds
120. relax clenched teeth	H. with a demonstration	h. in/for 30–60 seconds
121. inhibit teeth grinding	I. with verbal cues	i. in/for over 1 minute
122. inhibit grimacing	J. in the therapy setting	j. in/for — minutes
123. reduce excessive reaction to tactile stimulation of mouth/face	K. independently	k. 1 repetition
124. reduce excessive reaction to hot/cold stimulation of mouth/face	L. in functional activities	l. 2–5 repetitions
125. relax oral musculature		m. 6–10 repetitions
126. allow toothbrushing		n. over 10 repetitions
127. close lips		o. — repetitions
128. maintain lip closure		p. 0–5 feet
129. maintain lip closure to swallow		q. 5–15 feet
130. decrease drooling		r. 15–25 feet
		s. over 25 feet
		t. — feet
		u. to/at mid range/level
		v. to/at functional range/level
		w. to/at normal limits
		x. to/at —% of normal
		y. to/at — degrees

Normalization of Tone To Permit Oral Motor Functions continued

Behaviors	Conditions	Measurements
131. maintain the head in neutral to swallow 132. maintain proper alignment of jaw 133. maintain position of jaw with manual resistance 134. move jaw up and down 135. move jaw forward 136. move jaw laterally 137. demonstrate rotary movements of jaw 138. grade movements of jaw 139. maintain head and jaw stability with face/lip movements 140. demonstrate voluntary sucking 141. demonstrate blowing 142. demonstrate puckering 143. demonstrate smiling 144. maintain head and jaw stability with tongue movements 145. protrude the tongue 146. retract the tongue 147. elevate the tongue 148. depress the tongue	A. with maximum–moderate assistance B. with moderate–minimum assistance C. with __% assistance D. with guarding assistance E. with facilitation F. with tactile cues G. with proprioceptive cues H. with a demonstration I. with verbal cues J. in the therapy setting K. independently L. in functional activities	a. 1 out of 4 times b. 2 out of 4 times c. 3 out of 4 times d. 4 out of 4 times e. __% of the time f. in/for 0–5 seconds g. in/for 5–30 seconds h. in/for 30–60 seconds i. in/for over 1 minute j. in/for __ minutes k. 1 repetition l. 2–5 repetitions m. 6–10 repetitions n. over 10 repetitions o. __ repetitions p. 0–5 feet q. 5–15 feet r. 15–25 feet s. over 25 feet t. __ feet u. to/at mid range/level v. to/at functional range/level w. to/at normal limits x. to/at __% of normal y. to/at __ degrees

Normalization of Tone To Permit Oral Motor Functions continued

Behaviors	Conditions	Measurements
149. lateralize the tongue	A. with maximum–moderate assistance	a. 1 out of 4 times
150. suck from a bottle		b. 2 out of 4 times
151. maintain head in neutral to accept food	B. with moderate–minimum assistance	c. 3 out of 4 times
152. remove food from spoon with top lip closure	C. with __% assistance	d. 4 out of 4 times
	D. with guarding assistance	e. __% of the time
153. maintain head in neutral to drink	E. with facilitation	f. in/for 0–5 seconds
154. seal lips on cup to drink	F. with tactile cues	g. in/for 5–30 seconds
155. bite food	G. with proprioceptive cues	h. in/for 30–60 seconds
156. maintain head in neutral to bite food		i. in/for over 1 minute
157. chew food	H. with a demonstration	j. in/for __ minutes
158. maintain head in neutral to chew food	I. with verbal cues	k. 1 repetition
159. keep food in mouth while chewing	J. in the therapy setting	l. 2–5 repetitions
160. swallow easy textures of food (puréed, mashed, springy) without choking	K. independently	m. 6–10 repetitions
	L. in functional activities	n. over 10 repetitions
161. swallow difficult textures of food (slippery, crumbly, sticky) without choking		o. __ repetitions
		p. 0–5 feet
162. swallow liquids without choking		q. 5–15 feet
163. finger feed self		r. 15–25 feet
164. maintain head in neutral to finger feed		s. over 25 feet
165. feed self with spoon		t. __ feet
166. maintain head in neutral to feed self with spoon		u. to/at mid range/level
		v. to/at functional range/level
		w. to/at normal limits
		x. to/at __% of normal
		y. to/at __ degrees

Additional Objectives

Behaviors	Conditions	Measurements
The student will 167.	A. with maximum–moderate assistance B. with moderate–minimum assistance C. with __% assistance D. with guarding assistance E. with facilitation F. with tactile cues G. with proprioceptive cues H. with a demonstration I. with verbal cues J. in the therapy setting K. independently L. in functional activities	a. 1 out of 4 times b. 2 out of 4 times c. 3 out of 4 times d. 4 out of 4 times e. __% of the time f. in/for 0–5 seconds g. in/for 5–30 seconds h. in/for 30–60 seconds i. in/for over 1 minute j. in/for __ minutes k. 1 repetition l. 2–5 repetitions m. 6–10 repetitions n. over 10 repetitions o. __ repetitions p. 0–5 feet q. 5–15 feet r. 15–25 feet s. over 25 feet t. __ feet u. to/at mid range/level v. to/at functional range/level w. to/at normal limits x. to/at __% of normal y. to/at __ degrees

Righting and Equilibrium   II

Every movement involves a weight shift, and weight shifts are the stimulus for righting and equilibrium reactions. With displacement of the center of gravity (from movement of the body or the supporting surface), a group of automatic compensatory reactions occur that allow us to regain an antigravity posture while continuing to have freedom of movement.

Righting reactions restore the alignment of the head and neck with the trunk and are characterized by rotation within the body axis. It is not surprising that a righting reaction such as body righting on body is deficient in a developmentally disabled child, as it involves a coordinated flexion rotation pattern. Flexion precedes rotation developmentally, and if flexion never balances extension, normal rotation patterns will not develop.

Equilibrium reactions are complex whole body responses to a displacement of balance and their purpose is to bring the body's center of gravity over the base of support. They do not just maintain balance, but do so with specific movement components that generally include neck and trunk elongation on the weightbearing side, abduction-external rotation of the limbs, and trunk rotation.

Protective reactions are also part of the antigravity reflex mechanism and are used as safeguards in case balance is too far displaced for recovery. Instead of shifting the body away from the pull of gravity, they are used when falling into gravity and require proximal stability to be effective. Therefore, they are included in the next section, which is on proximal stability.

Development of Righting Reactions

Behaviors	Conditions	Measurements
The student will 1. demonstrate labyrinthine righting when held in space 2. demonstrate optical righting when held in space 3. demonstrate extension of legs and spine with thorax supported in space 4. demonstrate head righting against gravity with shoulders supported 5. demonstrate head righting against gravity with trunk supported 6. demonstrate head righting against gravity with pelvis supported 7. demonstrate head righting against gravity 8. demonstrate neck righting in supine 9. demonstrate body righting on head in supine 10. demonstrate body righting on body in supine 11. push with arm to roll from prone 12. roll from prone to sidelying 13. roll from prone to supine	A. with maximum–moderate assistance B. with moderate–minimum assistance C. with __% assistance D. with guarding assistance E. with facilitation F. with tactile cues G. with proprioceptive cues H. with a demonstration I. with verbal cues J. in the therapy setting K. independently L. in functional activities	a. 1 out of 4 times b. 2 out of 4 times c. 3 out of 4 times d. 4 out of 4 times e. __% of the time f in/for 0–5 seconds g. in/for 5–30 seconds h. in/for 30–60 seconds i. in/for over 1 minute j. in/for __ minutes k. 1 repetition l. 2–5 repetitions m. 6–10 repetitions n. over 10 repetitions o. __ repetitions p. 0–5 feet q. 5–15 feet r. 15–25 feet s. over 25 feet t. __ feet u. to/at mid range/level v. to/at functional range/level w. to/at normal limits x. to/at __% of normal y. to/at __ degrees

Development of Righting Reactions continued

Behaviors	Conditions	Measurements
14. roll from prone toward supine with flexion-rotation pattern 15. roll from prone toward supine with leg dissociation 16. roll segmentally from prone to supine 17. roll segmentally from prone to supine against manual resistance 18. grade segmental rolling from prone to supine 19. reach to roll from supine 20. pull self with dominant hand to roll from supine 21. pull self with nondominant hand to roll from supine 22. move arm across body to roll from supine 23. move leg across body to roll from supine 24. roll from supine to sidelying 25. maintain sidelying 26. bring hands together in sidelying 27. roll from supine to prone 28. roll from supine toward prone with flexion-rotation pattern	A. with maximum–moderate assistance B. with moderate–minimum assistance C. with __% assistance D. with guarding assistance E. with facilitation F. with tactile cues G. with proprioceptive cues H. with a demonstration I. with verbal cues J. in the therapy setting K. independently L. in functional activities	a. 1 out of 4 times b. 2 out of 4 times c. 3 out of 4 times d. 4 out of 4 times e. __% of the time f. in/for 0–5 seconds g. in/for 5–30 seconds h. in/for 30–60 seconds i. in/for over 1 minute j. in/for __ minutes k. 1 repetition l. 2–5 repetitions m. 6–10 repetitions n. over 10 repetitions o. __ repetitions p. 0–5 feet q. 5–15 feet r. 15–25 feet s. over 25 feet t. __ feet u. to/at mid range/level v. to/at functional range/level w. to/at normal limits x. to/at __% of normal y. to/at __ degrees

Development of Righting Reactions continued

Behaviors	Conditions	Measurements
29. roll from supine toward prone with leg dissociation 30. roll segmentally from supine to prone 31. roll segmentally against manual resistance from supine to prone 32. grade segmental rolling from supine to prone 33. bring arm from under body after rolling 34. flex arm, hip, and knee slightly with pelvis lifted on one side in prone 35. turn head to side with pelvis lifted on one side in prone 36. demonstrate an amphibian reaction 37. demonstrate body righting against gravity with pelvis supported 38. demonstrate body righting against gravity 39. roll from prone and rise to sitting 40. roll from supine and rise to sitting 41. right head and body against gravity to come to sitting 42. use flexion-rotation patterns to come to sitting 43. use flexion-rotation patterns in movement transitions	A. with maximum–moderate assistance B. with moderate–minimum assistance C. with __% assistance D. with guarding assistance E. with facilitation F. with tactile cues G. with proprioceptive cues H. with a demonstration I. with verbal cues J. in the therapy setting K. independently L. in functional activities	a. 1 out of 4 times b. 2 out of 4 times c. 3 out of 4 times d. 4 out of 4 times e. __% of the time f. in/for 0–5 seconds g. in/for 5–30 seconds h. in/for 30–60 seconds i. in/for over 1 minute j. in/for __ minutes k. 1 repetition l. 2–5 repetitions m. 6–10 repetitions n. over 10 repetitions o. __ repetitions p. 0–5 feet q. 5–15 feet r. 15–25 feet s. over 25 feet t. __ feet u. to/at mid range/level v. to/at functional range/level w. to/at normal limits x. to/at __% of normal y. to/at __ degrees

Demonstration of All Components of Equilibrium in Various Positions and Activities

Behaviors	Conditions	Measurements
The student will 44. right the head in response to a weight shift 45. demonstrate slight trunk flexion in response to a weight shift 46. demonstrate trunk rotation toward the nonweightbearing side in response to a weight shift 47. demonstrate trunk elongation on the weightbearing side in response to a weight shift 48. demonstrate trunk flexion-rotation-elongation in response to a weight shift 49. demonstrate shoulder flexion-abduction-external rotation in response to a weight shift 50. demonstrate hip flexion in response to a weight shift 51. demonstrate hip abduction in response to a weight shift 52. demonstrate hip external rotation in response to a weight shift 53. demonstrate hip flexion-abduction-external rotation in response to a weight shift	A. with maximum–moderate assistance B. with moderate–minimum assistance C. with __% assistance D. with guarding assistance E. with facilitation F. with tactile cues G. with proprioceptive cues H. with a demonstration I. with verbal cues J. in the therapy setting K. independently L. in functional activities	a. 1 out of 4 times b. 2 out of 4 times c. 3 out of 4 times d. 4 out of 4 times e. __% of the time f. in/for 0–5 seconds g. in/for 5–30 seconds h. in/for 30–60 seconds i. in/for over 1 minute j. in/for __ minutes k. 1 repetition l. 2–5 repetitions m. 6–10 repetitions n. over 10 repetitions o. __ repetitions p. 0–5 feet q. 5–15 feet r. 15–25 feet s. over 25 feet t. __ feet u. to/at mid range/level v. to/at functional range/level w. to/at normal limits x. to/at __% of normal y. to/at __ degrees

Demonstration of All Components of Equilibrium in Various Positions and Activities continued

Behaviors	Conditions	Measurements
54. demonstrate knee flexion in response to a weight shift 55. demonstrate ankle dorsiflexion in response to a weight shift 56. demonstrate all lower extremity components of equilibrium in response to a weight shift 57. demonstrate the _____ component of equilibrium in response to a weight shift in the _____ position 58. use an equilibrium reaction to maintain balance with a weight shift in prone 59. use an equilibrium reaction to maintain balance with a weight shift in supine 60. use an equilibrium reaction to maintain balance with a weight shift in sitting 61. use an equilibrium reaction to maintain balance with a weight shift in quadruped 62. demonstrate equilibrium reactions in creeping 63. demonstrate an equilibrium reaction in assuming the half-kneeling position 64. maintain half-kneeling with proper equilibrium	A. with maximum–moderate assistance B. with moderate–minimum assistance C. with __% assistance D. with guarding assistance E. with facilitation F. with tactile cues G. with proprioceptive cues H. with a demonstration I. with verbal cues J. in the therapy setting K. independently L. in functional activities	a. 1 out of 4 times b. 2 out of 4 times c. 3 out of 4 times d. 4 out of 4 times e. __% of the time f. in/for 0–5 seconds g. in/for 5–30 seconds h. in/for 30–60 seconds i. in/for over 1 minute j. in/for __ minutes k. 1 repetition l. 2–5 repetitions m. 6–10 repetitions n. over 10 repetitions o. __ repetitions p. 0–5 feet q. 5–15 feet r. 15–25 feet s. over 25 feet t. __ feet u. to/at mid range/level v. to/at functional range/level w. to/at normal limits x. to/at __% of normal y. to/at __ degrees

Demonstration of All Components of Equilibrium in Various Positions and Activities continued

Behaviors	Conditions	Measurements
65. use an equilibrium reaction to maintain balance with a weight shift in kneeling	A. with maximum–moderate assistance	a. 1 out of 4 times
66. demonstrate equilibrium reactions in kneel walking	B. with moderate–minimum assistance	b. 2 out of 4 times
67. use an equilibrium reaction to maintain balance with a weight shift in standing	C. with __% assistance	c. 3 out of 4 times
68. demonstrate an equilibrium reaction in raising one foot to a higher surface in standing	D. with guarding assistance	d. 4 out of 4 times
69. maintain standing with one foot on a higher surface with proper equilibrium	E. with facilitation	e. __% of the time
70. stand on one foot with proper equilibrium	F. with tactile cues	f. in/for 0–5 seconds
71. maintain equilibrium while performing dynamic activities in the _____ position	G. with proprioceptive cues	g. in/for 5–30 seconds
72. maintain equilibrium on an unstable surface in the _____ position	H. with a demonstration	h. in/for 30–60 seconds
73. maintain equilibrium while performing dynamic activities on an unstable surface in the _____ position	I. with verbal cues	i. in/for over 1 minute
74. actively shift weight in the _____ position	J. in the therapy setting	j. in/for __ minutes
75. shift weight to initiate movement transitions	K. independently	k. 1 repetition
76. shift weight for ADL	L. in functional activities	l. 2–5 repetitions
		m. 6–10 repetitions
		n. over 10 repetitions
		o. __ repetitions
		p. 0–5 feet
		q. 5–15 feet
		r. 15–25 feet
		s. over 25 feet
		t. __ feet
		u. to/at mid range/level
		v. to/at functional range/level
		w. to/at normal limits
		x. to/at __% of normal
		y. to/at __ degrees

Demonstration of All Components of Equilibrium in Various Positions and Activities continued

Behaviors	Conditions	Measurements
77. use equilibrium reactions to maintain sitting balance during dressing 78. use equilibrium reactions to maintain sitting balance on toilet 79. use equilibrium reactions to maintain sitting balance in bathtub 80. use equilibrium reactions to maintain balance while seated in classroom 81. use equilibrium reactions to maintain standing balance during dressing 82. maintain balance while stepping into bathtub 83. maintain balance during transitions between sitting and standing in bathtub 84. shift weight to initiate locomotion 85. demonstrate the _____ component of equilibrium in locomotion/gait 86. demonstrate equilibrium reactions in locomotion/gait 87. use equilibrium reactions to prevent falling while ambulating in school building 88. use equilibrium reactions to prevent falling while running on playground 89. use equilibrium reactions to prevent falling while using playground/P.E. equipment	A. with maximum–moderate assistance B. with moderate–minimum assistance C. with __% assistance D. with guarding assistance E. with facilitation F. with tactile cues G. with proprioceptive cues H. with a demonstration I. with verbal cues J. in the therapy setting K. independently L. in functional activities	a. 1 out of 4 times b. 2 out of 4 times c. 3 out of 4 times d. 4 out of 4 times e. __% of the time f. in/for 0–5 seconds g. in/for 5–30 seconds h. in/for 30–60 seconds i. in/for over 1 minute j. in/for __ minutes k. 1 repetition l. 2–5 repetitions m. 6–10 repetitions n. over 10 repetitions o. __ repetitions p. 0–5 feet q. 5–15 feet r. 15–25 feet s. over 25 feet t. __ feet u. to/at mid range/level v. to/at functional range/level w. to/at normal limits x. to/at __% of normal y. to/at __ degrees

Additional Objectives

Behaviors	Conditions	Measurements
The student will 90.	A. with maximum–moderate assistance B. with moderate–minimum assistance C. with __% assistance D. with guarding assistance E. with facilitation F. with tactile cues G. with proprioceptive cues H. with a demonstration I. with verbal cues J. in the therapy setting K. independently L. in functional activities	a. 1 out of 4 times b. 2 out of 4 times c. 3 out of 4 times d. 4 out of 4 times e. __% of the time f. in/for 0–5 seconds g. in/for 5–30 seconds h. in/for 30–60 seconds i. in/for over 1 minute j. in/for __ minutes k. 1 repetition l. 2–5 repetitions m. 6–10 repetitions n. over 10 repetitions o. __ repetitions p. 0–5 feet q. 5–15 feet r. 15–25 feet s. over 25 feet t. __ feet u. to/at mid range/level v. to/at functional range/level w. to/at normal limits x. to/at __% of normal y. to/at __ degrees

Proximal Stability   III

Proximal stability is the ability to stabilize in antigravity positions with simultaneous functional mobility. It requires a balance of flexor and extensor tone, the integration of muscle control in all positions, movement in all planes, weight shifts, symmetry, and equilibrium. Stability with functional mobility entails that the student can stabilize any body part to achieve movement of another (dissociation). Examples of dissociation include the following:

- dissociation of left from right lower extremity when half-kneeling or walking (pelvic stability to shift weight to and bear weight on one lower extremity while moving the other)
- dissociation of lower extremities from trunk and upper extremities when throwing (pelvic stability to fix lower extremities while twisting trunk and raising and flinging arm)
- dissociation of right fingers from right upper arm and wrist when typing and writing (shoulder girdle, elbow, and wrist stability with rapid finger movement)
- dissociation of head or trunk from jaw when chewing (head and trunk control as base for rotatory jaw movements)
- dissociation of hand or foot from rest of body when playing "Twister" (distal points are fixed while trunk moves over them)

Dissociation also includes postures or movements in which body parts can assume a variety of relationships to each other, without dominance of whole body patterns such as in the following examples:

- dissociation of left from right lower extremity when half-kneeling or standing with one foot on a higher surface (one hip is flexed, the other extended)
- dissociation of head from body when bridging (hyperextension posture of trunk with neck flexion)
- dissociation of head from limbs when head is turned to left with left elbow flexion (arm movements not dominated by ATNR)
- left from right upper extremity when rubbing stomach while patting head (arms are performing different motions in different positions)

Many developmentally disabled children keep their weight shifted to one side. They may even demonstrate an age level skill such as hopping on the less involved side while walking and sitting with grossly asymmetrical, poorly aligned patterns. Such asymmetry affects the whole body and precludes effective proximal stability.

The acme of proximal stability occurs when a child performs motor skills not only with stability, but with grading, which is the ability to move smoothly, accurately, and with control. If the child who demonstrates normal patterns, alignment, and equilibrium can also move slowly and accurately, he or she has achieved true functional mobility.

Practicing school skills without a solid base limits the progress that can be made; classroom, fine motor, prevocational, ADL, and playground skills all require good proximal stability. Fine motor and ADL skills specifically require shoulder girdle stability, which in turn depends on a stable base of trunk control and pelvic stability. Some fine motor activities and activities of daily living are included here, since they relate to this gross motor area. But they are not broken down extensively enough to reflect the cognitive, perceptual, sensory, and behavioral developments on which they also depend.

Demonstration of Stability with Proper Alignment in Upper Extremity Weightbearing

Behaviors	Conditions	Measurements
The student will 1. assume a prone on elbows position 2. maintain a prone on elbows position 3. maintain prone on elbows with head in neutral 4. maintain prone on elbows without shoulder hyperextension 5. maintain prone on elbows with relaxation of lower arms 6. maintain prone on elbows with head movements 7. shift weight to one side in prone on elbows position 8. reach with one arm in prone on elbows position 9. assume weight on one elbow in sideprop position 10. maintain weight on one elbow in sideprop position 11. right head in sideprop position 12. maintain weight on one elbow without shoulder hyperextension	A. with maximum–moderate assistance B. with moderate–minimum assistance C. with __% assistance D. with guarding assistance E. with facilitation F. with tactile cues G. with proprioceptive cues H. with a demonstration I. with verbal cues J. in the therapy setting K. independently L. in functional activities	a. 1 out of 4 times b. 2 out of 4 times c. 3 out of 4 times d. 4 out of 4 times e. __% of the time f. in/for 0–5 seconds g. in/for 5–30 seconds h. in/for 30–60 seconds i. in/for over 1 minute j. in/for __ minutes k. 1 repetition l. 2–5 repetitions m. 6–10 repetitions n. over 10 repetitions o. __ repetitions p. 0–5 feet q. 5–15 feet r. 15–25 feet s. over 25 feet t. __ feet u. to/at mid range/level v. to/at functional range/level w. to/at normal limits x. to/at __% of normal y. to/at __ degrees

Demonstration of Stability with Proper Alignment in Upper Extremity Weightbearing continued

Behaviors	Conditions	Measurements
13. maintain weight on one elbow with relaxation of lower arm	A. with maximum–moderate assistance	a. 1 out of 4 times
14. reach with opposite arm in sideprop position	B. with moderate–minimum assistance	b. 2 out of 4 times
15. maintain weight on one elbow with relaxation of legs	C. with __% assistance	c. 3 out of 4 times
16. assume weightbearing on hands in prone positions	D. with guarding assistance	d. 4 out of 4 times
17. maintain weight on hands in prone positions	E. with facilitation	e. __% of the time
18. maintain upper extremity weightbearing with head in neutral	F. with tactile cues	f. in/for 0–5 seconds
19. eliminate shoulder hyperextension in upper extremity weightbearing	G. with proprioceptive cues	g. in/for 5–30 seconds
20. eliminate elbow hyperextension in upper extremity weightbearing	H. with a demonstration	h. in/for 30–60 seconds
21. bear weight on ulnar side of palm	I. with verbal cues	i. in/for over 1 minute
22. bear weight with thumb and fingers extended	J. in the therapy setting	j. in/for __ minutes
23. maintain upper extremities in proper alignment in weightbearing	K. independently	k. 1 repetition
24. maintain upper extremity weightbearing with relaxation of legs	L. in functional activities	l. 2–5 repetitions
		m. 6–10 repetitions
		n. over 10 repetitions
		o. __ repetitions
		p. 0–5 feet
		q. 5–15 feet
		r. 15–25 feet
		s. over 25 feet
		t. __ feet
		u. to/at mid range/level
		v. to/at functional range/level
		w. to/at normal limits
		x. to/at __% of normal
		y. to/at __ degrees

Demonstration of Stability with Proper Alignment in Upper Extremity Weightbearing continued

Behaviors	Conditions	Measurements
25. maintain upper extremity weightbearing with head movements 26. shift weight to one side in upper extremity weightbearing 27. assume unilateral upper extremity weightbearing in prone positions 28. alternate left-right unilateral upper extremity weightbearing 29. maintain weightbearing on one arm while reaching with opposite arm 30. maintain weightbearing on one arm while crossing midline with opposite arm 31. maintain upper extremity weightbearing with trunk rotation. 32. move body over weightbearing arm 33. bear weight on upper extremities in back space 34. move between bear and crab positions over weightbearing upper extremity 35. grade movements between bear and crab positions 36. push with arm(s) to come to sitting	A. with maximum–moderate assistance B. with moderate–minimum assistance C. with __% assistance D. with guarding assistance E. with facilitation F. with tactile cues G. with proprioceptive cues H. with a demonstration I. with verbal cues J. in the therapy setting K. independently L. in functional activities	a. 1 out of 4 times b. 2 out of 4 times c. 3 out of 4 times d. 4 out of 4 times e. __% of the time f. in/for 0–5 seconds g. in/for 5–30 seconds h. in/for 30–60 seconds i. in/for over 1 minute j. in/for __ minutes k. 1 repetition l. 2–5 repetitions m. 6–10 repetitions n. over 10 repetitions o. __ repetitions p. 0–5 feet q. 5–15 feet r. 15–25 feet s. over 25 feet t. __ feet u. to/at mid range/level v. to/at functional range/level w. to/at normal limits x. to/at __% of normal y. to/at __ degrees

Demonstration of Stability with Proper Alignment in Upper Extremity Weightbearing continued

Behaviors	Conditions	Measurements
37. bear weight on hands in sitting 38. keep weight forward in sitting with upper extremity weightbearing 39. maintain sidesitting with upper extremity weightbearing 40. weight-bear on hand(s) in sitting with proper alignment of upper extremities 41. weight-bear on hands for support in lower extremity weightbearing	A. with maximum–moderate assistance B. with moderate–minimum assistance C. with __% assistance D. with guarding assistance E. with facilitation F. with tactile cues G. with proprioceptive cues H. with a demonstration I. with verbal cues J. in the therapy setting K. independently L. in functional activities	a. 1 out of 4 times b. 2 out of 4 times c. 3 out of 4 times d. 4 out of 4 times e. __% of the time f. in/for 0–5 seconds g. in/for 5–30 seconds h. in/for 00–00 seconds i. in/for over 1 minute j. in/for __ minutes k. 1 repetition l. 2–5 repetitions m. 6–10 repetitions n. over 10 repetitions o. __ repetitions p. 0–5 feet q. 5–15 feet r. 15–25 feet s. over 25 feet t. __ feet u. to/at mid range/level v. to/at functional range/level w. to/at normal limits x. to/at __% of normal y. to/at __ degrees

Quick Response for Functional Protective Reactions

Behaviors	Conditions	Measurements
The student will 42. brace the arm to prepare to bear weight with a forward balance displacement 43. brace the arm to prepare to bear weight with a lateral balance displacement 44. brace the arm to prepare to bear weight with a backward balance displacement 45. support body weight with arm to prevent falling 46. brace arms to prepare to bear weight in the parachute position 47. support body weight with arms to prevent falling in the parachute position 48. take a step to prevent falling with a balance displacement in standing 49. demonstrate functional protective reactions	A. with maximum–moderate assistance B. with moderate–minimum assistance C. with __% assistance D. with guarding assistance E. with facilitation F. with tactile cues G. with proprioceptive cues H. with a demonstration I. with verbal cues J. in the therapy setting K. independently L. in functional activities	a. 1 out of 4 times b. 2 out of 4 times c. 3 out of 4 times d. 4 out of 4 times e. __% of the time f. in/for 0–5 seconds g. in/for 5–30 seconds h. in/for 30–60 seconds i. in/for over 1 minute j. in/for __ minutes k. 1 repetition l. 2–5 repetitions m. 6–10 repetitions n. over 10 repetitions o. __ repetitions p. 0–5 feet q. 5–15 feet r. 15–25 feet s. over 25 feet t. __ feet u. to/at mid range/level v. to/at functional range/level w. to/at normal limits x. to/at __% of normal y. to/at __ degrees

Stabilization of Shoulder Girdle for Functional Mobility of Upper Extremities

Behaviors	Conditions	Measurements
The student will	A. with maximum–moderate assistance	a. 1 out of 4 times
50. stabilize shoulder girdle with relaxation of lower arm	B. with moderate–minimum assistance	b. 2 out of 4 times
	C. with __% assistance	c. 3 out of 4 times
51. stabilize shoulder girdle for elbow movements	D. with guarding assistance	d. 4 out of 4 times
52. stabilize shoulder girdle and elbow for forearm movements	E. with facilitation	e. __% of the time
	F. with tactile cues	f. in/for 0–5 seconds
53. stabilize shoulder girdle and elbow for wrist movements	G. with proprioceptive cues	g. in/for 5–30 seconds
	H. with a demonstration	h. in/for 30–60 seconds
54. stabilize shoulder girdle, elbow, and wrist for hand movements	I. with verbal cues	i. in/for over 1 minute
	J. in the therapy setting	j. in/for __ minutes
55. maintain shoulder girdle stability to grade upper extremity movement	K. independently	k. 1 repetition
	L. in functional activities	l. 2–5 repetitions
56. stabilize shoulder girdle to reach		m. 6–10 repetitions
57. stabilize shoulder girdle to reach down and forward		n. over 10 repetitions
		o. __ repetitions
58. stabilize shoulder girdle to reach forward at shoulder level		p. 0–5 feet
		q. 5–15 feet
59. stabilize shoulder girdle to reach to side		r. 15–25 feet
		s. over 25 feet
60. stabilize shoulder girdle to reach above		t. __ feet
61. stabilize shoulder girdle to reach behind		u. to/at mid range/level
		v. to/at functional range/level
62. stabilize shoulder girdle to reach with trunk rotation		w. to/at normal limits
		x. to/at __% of normal
		y. to/at __ degrees

Stabilization of Shoulder Girdle for Functional Mobility of Upper Extremities continued

Behaviors	Conditions	Measurements
63. stabilize shoulder girdle to reach and cross midline	A. with maximum–moderate assistance	a. 1 out of 4 times
64. stabilize shoulder girdle to reach with either hand	B. with moderate–minimum assistance	b. 2 out of 4 times
65. stabilize shoulder girdle to reach with both hands simultaneously	C. with __% assistance	c. 3 out of 4 times
66. stabilize shoulder girdle to reach in the _____ direction in the _____ position	D. with guarding assistance	d. 4 out of 4 times
67. stabilize shoulder girdle to reach with graded control	E. with facilitation	e. __% of the time
68. stabilize shoulder girdle to grasp	F. with tactile cues	f. in/for 0–5 seconds
69. stabilize shoulder girdle to pick up a large object with two hands	G. with proprioceptive cues	g. in/for 5–30 seconds
70. stabilize shoulder girdle to use a raking motion or grasp	H. with a demonstration	h. in/for 30–60 seconds
71. stabilize proximal joints to use an ulnar grasp	I. with verbal cues	i. in/for over 1 minute
72. stabilize proximal joints to use a palmar grasp in pronation	J. in the therapy setting	j. in/for __ minutes
73. stabilize proximal joints to use a palmar grasp with supination	K. independently	k. 1 repetition
74. stabilize proximal joints to use a radial palmar grasp	L. in functional activities	l. 2–5 repetitions
		m. 6–10 repetitions
		n. over 10 repetitions
		o. __ repetitions
		p. 0–5 feet
		q. 5–15 feet
		r. 15–25 feet
		s. over 25 feet
		t. __ feet
		u. to/at mid range/level
		v. to/at functional range/level
		w. to/at normal limits
		x. to/at __% of normal
		y. to/at __ degrees

Stabilization of Shoulder Girdle for Functional Mobility of Upper Extremities continued

Behaviors	Conditions	Measurements
75. stabilize proximal joints to use a radial digital grasp 76. stabilize proximal joints to use a tripod grasp 77. stabilize proximal joints to use an inferior pincer grasp 78. stabilize proximal joints to use a refined pincer grasp 79. stabilize proximal joints to show opposition of thumb to fingers 80. stabilize proximal joints to grasp with dominant hand 81. stabilize proximal joints to grasp with nondominant hand 82. stabilize proximal joints to use a _____ grasp with the _____ hand 83. stabilize shoulder girdle to use nondominant hand as an assist 84. stabilize shoulder girdle to poke or point at an object 85. stabilize shoulder girdle to transfer an object between hands	A. with maximum–moderate assistance B. with moderate–minimum assistance C. with __% assistance D. with guarding assistance E. with facilitation F. with tactile cues G. with proprioceptive cues H. with a demonstration I. with verbal cues J. in the therapy setting K. independently L. in functional activities	a. 1 out of 4 times b. 2 out of 4 times c. 3 out of 4 times d. 4 out of 4 times e. __% of the time f. in/for 0–5 seconds g. in/for 5–30 seconds h. in/for 30–60 seconds i. in/for over 1 minute j. in/for __ minutes k. 1 repetition l. 2–5 repetitions m. 6–10 repetitions n. over 10 repetitions o. __ repetitions p. 0–5 feet q. 5–15 feet r. 15–25 feet s. over 25 feet t. __ feet u. to/at mid range/level v. to/at functional range/level w. to/at normal limits x. to/at __% of normal y. to/at __ degrees

Stabilization of Shoulder Girdle for Functional Mobility of Upper Extremities continued

Behaviors	Conditions	Measurements
86. stabilize proximal joints to hold an object with one hand while manipulating it with the other	A. with maximum– moderate assistance	a. 1 out of 4 times
87. stabilize proximal joints to demonstrate in-hand manipulation	B. with moderate– minimum assistance	b. 2 out of 4 times
88. stabilize shoulder girdle to release	C. with __% assistance	c. 3 out of 4 times
89. stabilize shoulder girdle to release an object without accuracy	D. with guarding assistance	d. 4 out of 4 times
90. stabilize shoulder girdle to release an object with accuracy	E. with facilitation	e. __% of the time
91. stabilize shoulder girdle to place an object without accuracy	F. with tactile cues	f. in/for 0–5 seconds
92. stabilize shoulder girdle to place an object with accuracy	G. with proprioceptive cues	g. in/for 5–30 seconds
93. stabilize shoulder girdle to release an object from the nondominant hand	H. with a demonstration	h. in/for 30–60 seconds
94. stabilize shoulder girdle to release an object quickly with accuracy	I. with verbal cues	i. in/for over 1 minute
95. stabilize shoulder girdle for support in toileting	J. in the therapy setting	j. in/for __ minutes
96. stabilize shoulder girdle to hold front support bar during toileting	K. independently	k. 1 repetition
97. stabilize shoulder girdle to reach for and hold grab bars during toileting	L. in functional activities	l. 2–5 repetitions
		m. 6–10 repetitions
		n. over 10 repetitions
		o. __ repetitions
		p. 0–5 feet
		q. 5–15 feet
		r. 15–25 feet
		s. over 25 feet
		t. __ feet
		u. to/at mid range/level
		v. to/at functional range/level
		w. to/at normal limits
		x. to/at __% of normal
		y. to/at __ degrees

Stabilization of Shoulder Girdle for Functional Mobility of Upper Extremities continued

Behaviors	*Conditions*	*Measurements*
98. stabilize shoulder girdle to reach behind to hold grab bars during toiletting 99. stabilize shoulder girdle to adjust clothing in preparation for toiletting 100. stabilize shoulder girdle to adjust clothing following toiletting 101. stabilize shoulder girdle to wipe self from front after using toilet 102. stabilize shoulder girdle to wipe self from back after using toilet 103. stabilize shoulder girdle to put on and remove sanitary pads 104. stabilize shoulder girdle for self-feeding 105. stabilize shoulder girdle to finger feed self 106. stabilize shoulder girdle to feed self with spoon with spilling 107. stabilize shoulder girdle to feed self with spoon without spilling 108. stabilize shoulder girdle to feed self with adaptive spoon 109. stabilize shoulder girdle to scoop with spoon	A. with maximum–moderate assistance B. with moderate–minimum assistance C. with __% assistance D. with guarding assistance E. with facilitation F. with tactile cues G. with proprioceptive cues H. with a demonstration I. with verbal cues J. in the therapy setting K. independently L. in functional activities	a. 1 out of 4 times b. 2 out of 4 times c. 3 out of 4 times d. 4 out of 4 times e. __% of the time f. in/for 0–5 seconds g. in/for 5–30 seconds h. in/for 30–60 seconds i. in/for over 1 minute j. in/for __ minutes k. 1 repetition l. 2–5 repetitions m. 6–10 repetitions n. over 10 repetitions o. __ repetitions p. 0–5 feet q. 5–15 feet r. 15–25 feet s. over 25 feet t. __ feet u. to/at mid range/level v. to/at functional range/level w. to/at normal limits x. to/at __% of normal y. to/at __ degrees

Stabilization of Shoulder Girdle for Functional Mobility of Upper Extremities continued

Behaviors	Conditions	Measurements
110. stabilize shoulder girdle to bring cup to mouth with spilling 111. stabilize shoulder girdle to bring cup to mouth without spilling 112. stabilize shoulder girdle for grooming activities 113. stabilize shoulder girdle to hold and raise toothbrush to mouth 114. stabilize shoulder girdle to put toothpaste on a toothbrush 115. stabilize shoulder girdle to use a toothbrush 116. stabilize shoulder girdle to wash hands 117. stabilize shoulder girdle to dry hands 118. stabilize shoulder girdle to hold a washcloth 119. stabilize shoulder girdle to wash face with a washcloth 120. stabilize shoulder girdle to turn a faucet on and off 121. stabilize proximal joints to hold a comb or brush	A. with maximum–moderate assistance B. with moderate–minimum assistance C. with __% assistance D. with guarding assistance E. with facilitation F. with tactile cues G. with proprioceptive cues H. with a demonstration I. with verbal cues J. in the therapy setting K. independently L. in functional activities	a. 1 out of 4 times b. 2 out of 4 times c. 3 out of 4 times d. 4 out of 4 times e. __% of the time f. in/for 0–5 seconds g. in/for 5–30 seconds h. in/for 30–60 seconds i. in/for over 1 minute j. in/for __ minutes k. 1 repetition l. 2–5 repetitions m. 6–10 repetitions n. over 10 repetitions o. __ repetitions p. 0–5 feet q. 5–15 feet r. 15–25 feet s. over 25 feet t. __ feet u. to/at mid range/level v. to/at functional range/level w. to/at normal limits x. to/at __% of normal y. to/at __ degrees

Stabilization of Shoulder Girdle for Functional Mobility of Upper Extremities continued

Behaviors	Conditions	Measurements
122. stabilize shoulder girdle to raise arm to back of head for combing or brushing	A. with maximum–moderate assistance	a. 1 out of 4 times
123. stabilize shoulder girdle to comb or brush hair	B. with moderate–minimum assistance	b. 2 out of 4 times c. 3 out of 4 times d. 4 out of 4 times
124. stabilize shoulder girdle to wash body while sitting in a chair	C. with __% assistance D. with guarding assistance	e. __% of the time f. in/for 0–5 seconds g. in/for 5–30 seconds
125. stabilize shoulder girdle to wash body while sitting in a bathtub	E. with facilitation F. with tactile cues	h. in/for 30–60 seconds i. in/for over 1 minute
126. stabilize shoulder girdle for self-dressing	G. with proprioceptive cues	j. in/for __ minutes k. 1 repetition
127. dissociate body parts for dressing activities	H. with a demonstration I. with verbal cues	l. 2–5 repetitions m. 6–10 repetitions
128. bring hands together for dressing activities	J. in the therapy setting	n. over 10 repetitions
129. hold arm out for dressing	K. independently	o. __ repetitions
130. hold leg/foot out for dressing	L. in functional activities	p. 0–5 feet
131. push arms through sleeves		q. 5–15 feet
132. push legs through pants		r. 15–25 feet
133. stabilize shoulder girdle to remove hat		s. over 25 feet t. __ feet
134. stabilize shoulder girdle to put on hat		u. to/at mid range/level
135. stabilize shoulder girdle to remove shoes and socks		v. to/at functional range/level
136. stabilize shoulder girdle to push bottom garment down past buttocks		w. to/at normal limits x. to/at __% of normal y. to/at __ degrees

Stabilization of Shoulder Girdle for Functional Mobility of Upper Extremities continued

Behaviors	Conditions	Measurements
137. stabilize shoulder girdle to remove coat	A. with maximum–moderate assistance	a. 1 out of 4 times
138. stabilize shoulder girdle to remove tops with front opening	B. with moderate–minimum assistance	b. 2 out of 4 times
139. stabilize shoulder girdle to remove pants	C. with __% assistance	c. 3 out of 4 times
140. stabilize shoulder girdle to remove tops over the head	D. with guarding assistance	d. 4 out of 4 times
141. stabilize shoulder girdle to remove underclothing	E. with facilitation	e. __% of the time
142. stabilize shoulder girdle to put on tops over the head	F. with tactile cues	f. in/for 0–5 seconds
143. stabilize shoulder girdle to put on coat	G. with proprioceptive cues	g. in/for 5–30 seconds
144. stabilize shoulder girdle to put on tops with front opening	H. with a demonstration	h. in/for 30–60 seconds
145. stabilize shoulder girdle to put on underclothing	I. with verbal cues	i. in/for over 1 minute
146. stabilize shoulder girdle to put on pants	J. in the therapy setting	j. in/for __ minutes
147. stabilize shoulder girdle to put on shoes	K. independently	k. 1 repetition
148. stabilize shoulder girdle to put on socks	L. in functional activities	l. 2–5 repetitions
149. stabilize shoulder girdle to undo fastenings		m. 6–10 repetitions
150. stabilize shoulder girdle to undo a _____ type fastening		n. over 10 repetitions
		o. __ repetitions
		p. 0–5 feet
		q. 5–15 feet
		r. 15–25 feet
		s. over 25 feet
		t. __ feet
		u. to/at mid range/level
		v. to/at functional range/level
		w. to/at normal limits
		x. to/at __% of normal
		y. to/at __ degrees

Stabilization of Shoulder Girdle for Functional Mobility of Upper Extremities continued

Behaviors	Conditions	Measurements
151. stabilize shoulder girdle to undo fastenings on own clothing	A. with maximum–moderate assistance	a. 1 out of 4 times
152. stabilize shoulder girdle to undo a _____ type fastening on own clothing	B. with moderate–minimum assistance	b. 2 out of 4 times
	C. with __% assistance	c. 3 out of 4 times
153. stabilize shoulder girdle to do up fastenings	D. with guarding assistance	d. 4 out of 4 times
154. stabilize shoulder girdle to do up a _____ type fastening	E. with facilitation	e. __% of the time
	F. with tactile cues	f. in/for 0–5 seconds
	G. with proprioceptive cues	g. in/for 5–30 seconds
155. stabilize shoulder girdle to do up fastenings on own clothing		h. in/for 30–60 seconds
	H. with a demonstration	i. in/for over 1 minute
156. stabilize shoulder girdle to do up a _____ type fastening on own clothing	I. with verbal cues	j. in/for __ minutes
	J. in the therapy setting	k. 1 repetition
157. stabilize shoulder girdle to tie shoes	K. independently	l. 2–5 repetitions
	L. in functional activities	m. 6–10 repetitions
158. maintain shoulder girdle stability for control in fine motor activities		n. over 10 repetitions
		o. __ repetitions
159. maintain shoulder girdle stability for control in bilateral fine motor activities		p. 0–5 feet
		q. 5–15 feet
		r. 15–25 feet
160. stabilize shoulder girdle for control in the fine motor activity _____		s. over 25 feet
		t. __ feet
161. stabilize proximal joints for control in holding a writing utensil with an immature grasp		u. to/at mid range/level
		v. to/at functional range/level
		w. to/at normal limits
		x. to/at __% of normal
		y. to/at __ degrees

Stabilization of Shoulder Girdle for Functional Mobility of Upper Extremities continued

Behaviors	Conditions	Measurements
162. stabilize proximal joints for control in holding a writing utensil with a digital grasp	A. with maximum–moderate assistance	a. 1 out of 4 times
163. stabilize proximal joints for control in holding a writing utensil with a mature grasp	B. with moderate–minimum assistance	b. 2 out of 4 times
164. stabilize proximal joints for control in using a writing utensil	C. with __% assistance	c. 3 out of 4 times
165. stabilize proximal joints for control in holding adaptive scissors	D. with guarding assistance	d. 4 out of 4 times
166. stabilize proximal joints for control in opening and closing adaptive scissors	E. with facilitation	e. __% of the time
167. stabilize proximal joints for control in cutting with adaptive scissors	F. with tactile cues	f. in/for 0–5 seconds
168. stabilize proximal joints for control in holding standard scissors	G. with proprioceptive cues	g. in/for 5–30 seconds
169. stabilize proximal joints for control in opening and closing standard scissors	H. with a demonstration	h. in/for 30–60 seconds
170. stabilize proximal joints for control in cutting with standard scissors	I. with verbal cues	i. in/for over 1 minute
	J. in the therapy setting	j. in/for __ minutes
	K. independently	k. 1 repetition
	L. in functional activities	l. 2–5 repetitions
		m. 6–10 repetitions
		n. over 10 repetitions
		o. __ repetitions
		p. 0–5 feet
		q. 5–15 feet
		r. 15–25 feet
		s. over 25 feet
		t. __ feet
		u. to/at mid range/level
		v. to/at functional range/level
		w. to/at normal limits
		x. to/at __% of normal
		y. to/at __ degrees

Demonstration of Stability with Proper Alignment in Sitting

Behaviors	Conditions	Measurements
The student will		
171. come to sitting from prone	A. with maximum–moderate assistance	a. 1 out of 4 times
172. come to sitting from supine		b. 2 out of 4 times
173. come to sitting from sidelying	B. with moderate–minimum assistance	c. 3 out of 4 times
174. roll to sidelying in preparation for coming to sit	C. with __% assistance	d. 4 out of 4 times
175. use upper extremities to push to sitting	D. with guarding assistance	e. __% of the time
		f. in/for 0–5 seconds
176. use flexion-rotation patterns to come to sitting	E. with facilitation	g. in/for 5–30 seconds
	F. with tactile cues	h. in/for 30–60 seconds
177. come to sitting with graded control	G. with proprioceptive cues	i. in/for over 1 minute
178. assume prop sitting	H. with a demonstration	j. in/for __ minutes
179. assume sitting over edge of bed or table	I. with verbal cues	k. 1 repetition
180. assume ring sitting	J. in the therapy setting	l. 2–5 repetitions
181. assume longsitting	K. independently	m. 6–10 repetitions
182. assume tailor sitting	L. in functional activities	n. over 10 repetitions
183. assume sidesitting		o. __ repetitions
184. assume sidesitting on nondominant side		p. 0–5 feet
185. assume _____ sitting with graded control		q. 5–15 feet
		r. 15–25 feet
186. grade movement transition from sitting to floor		s. over 25 feet
		t. __ feet
187. maintain prop sitting		u. to/at mid range/level
		v. to/at functional range/level
		w. to/at normal limits
		x. to/at __% of normal
		y. to/at __ degrees

Demonstration of Stability with Proper Alignment in Sitting continued

Behaviors	Conditions	Measurements
188. maintain ring sitting	A. with maximum–moderate assistance	a. 1 out of 4 times
189. maintain longsitting		b. 2 out of 4 times
190. longsit without a posterior pelvic tilt	B. with moderate–minimum assistance	c. 3 out of 4 times
191. maintain tailor sitting	C. with __% assistance	d. 4 out of 4 times
192. maintain sidesitting	D. with guarding assistance	e. __% of the time
193. assume and maintain sidesitting on the nonpreferred side	E. with facilitation	f. in/for 0–5 seconds
	F. with tactile cues	g. in/for 5–30 seconds
194. eliminate W sitting	G. with proprioceptive cues	h. in/for 30–60 seconds
195. maintain stability in chair or bolster sitting	H. with a demonstration	i. in/for over 1 minute
196. maintain stability seated on an adaptive toilet	I. with verbal cues	j. in/for __ minutes
	J. in the therapy setting	k. 1 repetition
197. maintain stability seated on a standard toilet	K. independently	l. 2–5 repetitions
	L. in functional activities	m. 6–10 repetitions
198. maintain stability seated in a bathtub		n. over 10 repetitions
199. maintain head in neutral in sitting		o. __ repetitions
200. maintain trunk in neutral in sitting		p. 0–5 feet
201. maintain the pelvis in neutral in sitting		q. 5–15 feet
202. maintain stability in sitting with relaxation of arms		r. 15–25 feet
		s. over 25 feet
203. shift weight to midline in sitting		t. __ feet
		u. to/at mid range/level
		v. to/at functional range/level
		w. to/at normal limits
		x. to/at __% of normal
		y. to/at __ degrees

Demonstration of Stability with Proper Alignment in Sitting continued

Behaviors	Conditions	Measurements
204. bring head, shoulders, and trunk into alignment over the base of support in sitting	A. with maximum–moderate assistance	a. 1 out of 4 times
	B. with moderate–minimum assistance	b. 2 out of 4 times
205. maintain stability in sitting with head movements	C. with __% assistance	c. 3 out of 4 times
	D. with guarding assistance	d. 4 out of 4 times
206. maintain stability in sitting with trunk movements	E. with facilitation	e. __% of the time
	F. with tactile cues	f. in/for 0–5 seconds
207. maintain stability in sitting with upper extremity movements	G. with proprioceptive cues	g. in/for 5–30 seconds
	H. with a demonstration	h. in/for 30–60 seconds
208. maintain stability in sitting for ADL	I. with verbal cues	i. in/for over 1 minute
	J. in the therapy setting	j. in/for __ minutes
209. maintain stability in sitting for fine motor activities	K. independently	k. 1 repetition
	L. in functional activities	l. 2–5 repetitions
210. move from one sitting position to another		m. 6–10 repetitions
		n. over 10 repetitions
211. use flexion-rotation patterns between various sitting positions		o. __ repetitions
		p. 0–5 feet
212. grade movement transition between various sitting positions		q. 5–15 feet
		r. 15–25 feet
213. seat self in an optimum position for classroom activities		s. over 25 feet
		t. __ feet
		u. to/at mid range/level
		v. to/at functional range/level
		w. to/at normal limits
		x. to/at __% of normal
		y. to/at __ degrees

Demonstration of Stability with Proper Alignment in Lower Extremity Weightbearing

Behaviors	Conditions	Measurements
The student will 214. assume a quadruped position 215. assume quadruped from sidesitting 216. grade transitions between sidesitting and quadruped 217. maintain a quadruped position 218. maintain head in neutral in quadruped 219. maintain stability in quadruped with head movements 220. maintain quadruped with proper alignment of limbs 221. weight-bear on ulnar side of open palms in quadruped 222. maintain the pelvis in neutral in quadruped 223. maintain quadruped against manual resistance 224. shift weight to midline in quadruped 225. shift weight to nonpreferred side in quadruped 226. shift weight to alternate limbs in quadruped	A. with maximum–moderate assistance B. with moderate–minimum assistance C. with __% assistance D. with guarding assistance E. with facilitation F. with tactile cues G. with proprioceptive cues H. with a demonstration I. with verbal cues J. in the therapy setting K. independently L. in functional activities	a. 1 out of 4 times b. 2 out of 4 times c. 3 out of 4 times d. 4 out of 4 times e. __% of the time f. in/for 0–5 seconds g. in/for 5–30 seconds h. in/for 30–60 seconds i. in/for over 1 minute j. in/for __ minutes k. 1 repetition l. 2–5 repetitions m. 6–10 repetitions n. over 10 repetitions o. __ repetitions p. 0–5 feet q. 5–15 feet r. 15–25 feet s. over 25 feet t. __ feet u. to/at mid range/level v. to/at functional range/level w. to/at normal limits x. to/at __% of normal y. to/at __ degrees

Demonstration of Stability with Proper Alignment in Lower Extremity Weightbearing continued

Behaviors	Conditions	Measurements
227. extend alternate arms in quadruped 228. shift weight to alternate arms in quadruped for fine motor activities 229. extend alternate legs in quadruped 230. flex alternate hips in quadruped 231. flex one hip to bring foot into a weightbearing position in quadruped 232. push from quadruped to bear position 233. grade movement transitions between quadruped and bear positions 234. assume an upright kneeling position 235. push to kneeling with shoulder girdle stability 236. assume kneeling without hyperextension thrust 237. grade movement transitions between quadruped and kneeling 238. support weight in upright kneeling with properly aligned upper extremities 239. maintain an upright kneeling position 240. maintain upright kneeling with head in neutral	A. with maximum–moderate assistance B. with moderate–minimum assistance C. with __% assistance D. with guarding assistance E. with facilitation F. with tactile cues G. with proprioceptive cues H. with a demonstration I. with verbal cues J. in the therapy setting K. independently L. in functional activities	a. 1 out of 4 times b. 2 out of 4 times c. 3 out of 4 times d. 4 out of 4 times e. __% of the time f. in/for 0–5 seconds g. in/for 5–30 seconds h. in/for 30–60 seconds i. in/for over 1 minute j. in/for __ minutes k. 1 repetition l. 2–5 repetitions m. 6–10 repetitions n. over 10 repetitions o. __ repetitions p. 0–5 feet q. 5–15 feet r. 15–25 feet s. over 25 feet t. __ feet u. to/at mid range/level v. to/at functional range/level w. to/at normal limits x. to/at __% of normal y. to/at __ degrees

Demonstration of Stability with Proper Alignment in Lower Extremity Weightbearing continued

Behaviors	Conditions	Measurements
241. maintain upright kneeling with trunk in neutral 242. maintain the pelvis in neutral in upright kneeling 243. maintain stability in kneeling with relaxation of arms 244. maintain stability in kneeling with head movements 245. maintain stability in kneeling with trunk movements 246. maintain stability in kneeling with arm movements 247. maintain stability in kneeling during fine motor activities 248. maintain stability in kneeling during dynamic activities 249. maintain upright kneeling against manual resistance 250. shift weight to midline in kneeling 251. shift weight to nonpreferred side in kneeling 252. assume a half-kneeling position	A. with maximum–moderate assistance B. with moderate–minimum assistance C. with __% assistance D. with guarding assistance E. with facilitation F. with tactile cues G. with proprioceptive cues H. with a demonstration I. with verbal cues J. in the therapy setting K. independently L. in functional activities	a. 1 out of 4 times b. 2 out of 4 times c. 3 out of 4 times d. 4 out of 4 times e. __% of the time f. in/for 0–5 seconds g. in/for 5–30 seconds h. in/for 30–60 seconds i. in/for over 1 minute j. in/for __ minutes k. 1 repetition l. 2–5 repetitions m. 6–10 repetitions n. over 10 repetitions o. __ repetitions p. 0–5 feet q. 5–15 feet r. 15–25 feet s. over 25 feet t. __ feet u. to/at mid range/level v. to/at functional range/level w. to/at normal limits x. to/at __% of normal y. to/at __ degrees

Demonstration of Stability with Proper Alignment in Lower Extremity Weightbearing continued

Behaviors	Conditions	Measurements
253. assume half-kneeling on the nonpreferred side	A. with maximum–moderate assistance	a. 1 out of 4 times
254. use flexion-rotation pattern to assume half-kneeling	B. with moderate–minimum assistance	b. 2 out of 4 times
		c. 3 out of 4 times
		d. 4 out of 4 times
255. grade transitions between kneeling and half-kneeling	C. with __% assistance	e. __% of the time
	D. with guarding assistance	f. in/for 0–5 seconds
		g. in/for 5–30 seconds
256. assume half-kneeling against manual resistance	E. with facilitation	h. in/for 30–60 seconds
	F. with tactile cues	i. in/for over 1 minute
257. support weight in half-kneeling with properly aligned upper extremities	G. with proprioceptive cues	j. in/for __ minutes
		k. 1 repetition
	H. with a demonstration	l. 2–5 repetitions
258. maintain a half-kneeling position	I. with verbal cues	m. 6–10 repetitions
259. maintain half-kneeling on the nonpreferred side	J. in the therapy setting	n. over 10 repetitions
	K. independently	o. __ repetitions
260. maintain half-kneeling with head in neutral	L. in functional activities	p. 0–5 feet
		q. 5–15 feet
		r. 15–25 feet
261. half-kneel with the pelvis in neutral		s. over 25 feet
262. half-kneel with proper positioning of the raised leg		t. __ feet
		u. to/at mid range/level
263. maintain half-kneeling with relaxation of arms		v. to/at functional range/level
		w. to/at normal limits
264. maintain stability in half-kneeling with head movements		x. to/at __% of normal
		y. to/at __ degrees

Demonstration of Stability with Proper Alignment in Lower Extremity Weightbearing continued

Behaviors	Conditions	Measurements
265. maintain stability in half-kneeling with trunk movements	A. with maximum–moderate assistance	a. 1 out of 4 times
266. maintain stability in half-kneeling with arm movements	B. with moderate–minimum assistance	b. 2 out of 4 times
267. maintain stability in half-kneeling during fine motor activities	C. with __% assistance	c. 3 out of 4 times
268. maintain lower extremity dissociation and alignment in half-kneeling during dynamic activities	D. with guarding assistance	d. 4 out of 4 times
269. maintain stability in half-kneeling during dynamic activities	E. with facilitation	e. __% of the time
270. come to partial standing from bolster sitting	F. with tactile cues	f. in/for 0–5 seconds
271. keep weight forward in bolster sit to stand	G. with proprioceptive cues	g. in/for 5–30 seconds
272. bear weight on lateral borders of feet in bolster sit to stand	H. with a demonstration	h. in/for 30–60 seconds
273. grade bolster sit to stand	I. with verbal cues	i. in/for over 1 minute
274. pull or push to stand	J. in the therapy setting	j. in/for __ minutes
275. pull or push to stand without hyperextension thrust	K. independently	k. 1 repetition
276. pull or push to stand with weight forward	L. in functional activities	l. 2–5 repetitions
277. push to stand with shoulder girdle stability		m. 6–10 repetitions
		n. over 10 repetitions
		o. __ repetitions
		p. 0–5 feet
		q. 5–15 feet
		r. 15–25 feet
		s. over 25 feet
		t. __ feet
		u. to/at mid range/level
		v. to/at functional range/level
		w. to/at normal limits
		x. to/at __% of normal
		y. to/at __ degrees

Demonstration of Stability with Proper Alignment in Lower Extremity Weightbearing continued

Behaviors	Conditions	Measurements
278. assume a standing position	A. with maximum–moderate assistance	a. 1 out of 4 times
279. rise to standing from chair sitting		b. 2 out of 4 times
280. keep weight forward in rising from chair sitting	B. with moderate–minimum assistance	c. 3 out of 4 times
	C. with __% assistance	d. 4 out of 4 times
281. grade movement transitions between chair sitting and standing	D. with guarding assistance	e. __% of the time
		f. in/for 0–5 seconds
282. assume standing through half-kneeling	E. with facilitation	g. in/for 5–30 seconds
	F. with tactile cues	h. in/for 30–60 seconds
283. keep weight forward in coming to stand through half-kneeling	G. with proprioceptive cues	i. in/for over 1 minute
		j. in/for __ minutes
284. grade transitions between kneeling and standing	H. with a demonstration	k. 1 repetition
	I. with verbal cues	l. 2–5 repetitions
285. support weight in standing with properly aligned upper extremities	J. in the therapy setting	m. 6–10 repetitions
	K. independently	n. over 10 repetitions
286. maintain a standing position	L. in functional activities	o. __ repetitions
287. maintain standing with head in neutral		p. 0–5 feet
288. maintain standing with trunk in neutral		q. 5–15 feet
289. maintain standing with pelvis in neutral		r. 15–25 feet
290. maintain standing with relaxation of arms		s. over 25 feet
291. stand without knee hyperextension		t. __ feet
292. bear weight on lateral borders of feet in standing		u. to/at mid range/level
		v. to/at functional range/level
		w. to/at normal limits
		x. to/at __% of normal
		y. to/at __ degrees

Demonstration of Stability with Proper Alignment in Lower Extremity Weightbearing continued

Behaviors	Conditions	Measurements
293. maintain stability in standing with head movements	A. with maximum–moderate assistance	a. 1 out of 4 times
294. maintain stability in standing with trunk movements	B. with moderate–minimum assistance	b. 2 out of 4 times c. 3 out of 4 times d. 4 out of 4 times
295. maintain stability in standing with arm movements	C. with __% assistance D. with guarding assistance	e. __% of the time f. in/for 0–5 seconds
296. maintain stability in standing during fine motor activities	E. with facilitation F. with tactile cues	g. in/for 5–30 seconds h. in/for 30–60 seconds i. in/for over 1 minute
297. maintain stability in standing during dynamic activities	G. with proprioceptive cues	j. in/for __ minutes k. 1 repetition
298. shift weight to midline in standing	H. with a demonstration I. with verbal cues	l. 2–5 repetitions m. 6–10 repetitions
299. shift weight to the nonpreferred side in standing	J. in the therapy setting K. independently	n. over 10 repetitions o. __ repetitions
300. bring the head, shoulders, trunk, and pelvis into alignment over the base of support in standing	L. in functional activities	p. 0–5 feet q. 5–15 feet r. 15–25 feet s. over 25 feet
301. maintain standing against manual resistance		t. __ feet u. to/at mid range/level
302. move body over weightbearing leg		v. to/at functional range/level
303. maintain pelvic stability with lower extremity mobility		w. to/at normal limits x. to/at __% of normal
304. maintain pelvic stability to grade lower extremity movement		y. to/at __ degrees

Demonstration of Stability with Proper Alignment in Lower Extremity Weightbearing continued

Behaviors	*Conditions*	*Measurements*
305. stand with one foot on higher surface	A. with maximum–moderate assistance	a. 1 out of 4 times
306. stand on one foot	B. with moderate–minimum assistance	b. 2 out of 4 times
307. stand on one foot without hyperextension posturing	C. with ___% assistance	c. 3 out of 4 times
308. stand on one foot with relaxation of arms	D. with guarding assistance	d. 4 out of 4 times
309. stand on one foot for dressing activities	E. with facilitation	e. ___% of the time
310. step into a bathtub	F. with tactile cues	f. in/for 0–5 seconds
311. grade transitions between sitting and standing in a bathtub	G. with proprioceptive cues	g. in/for 5–30 seconds
	H. with a demonstration	h. in/for 30–60 seconds
	I. with verbal cues	i. in/for over 1 minute
	J. in the therapy setting	j. in/for ___ minutes
	K. independently	k. 1 repetition
	L. in functional activities	l. 2–5 repetitions
		m. 6–10 repetitions
		n. over 10 repetitions
		o. ___ repetitions
		p. 0–5 feet
		q. 5–15 feet
		r. 15–25 feet
		s. over 25 feet
		t. ___ feet
		u. to/at mid range/level
		v. to/at functional range/level
		w. to/at normal limits
		x. to/at ___% of normal
		y. to/at ___ degrees

Additional Objectives

Behaviors	Conditions	Measurements
The student will 312.	A. with maximum–moderate assistance B. with moderate–minimum assistance C. with __% assistance D. with guarding assistance E. with facilitation F. with tactile cues G. with proprioceptive cues H. with a demonstration I. with verbal cues J. in the therapy setting K. independently L. in functional activities	a. 1 out of 4 times b. 2 out of 4 times c. 3 out of 4 times d. 4 out of 4 times e. __% of the time f. in/for 0–5 seconds g. in/for 5–30 seconds h. in/for 30–60 seconds i. in/for over 1 minute j. in/for __ minutes k. 1 repetition l. 2–5 repetitions m. 6–10 repetitions n. over 10 repetitions o. __ repetitions p. 0–5 feet q. 5–15 feet r. 15–25 feet s. over 25 feet t. __ feet u. to/at mid range/level v. to/at functional range/level w. to/at normal limits x. to/at __% of normal y. to/at __ degrees

Locomotion and Gait IV

Locomotion is a major milestone for a child, because it represents independence. Normal crawling, creeping, and walking incorporate proximal stability, equilibrium, dissociation, and grading; all combine for energy-efficient locomotion that maximizes endurance and function. Locomotion with poor quality movement patterns is inefficient, tiring, unattractive, and even dangerous. Inhibiting abnormal tone and patterns and facilitating normal components lay the base for functional locomotion.

The use of adaptive equipment, assistive devices, or orthotics may block certain components of a normal gait pattern. For example, pushing a rollator interferes with trunk rotation and arm swing. Long leg braces block knee flexion and ankle dorsal flexion or plantar flexion. Seated walkers throw off the entire weightbearing and equilibrium mechanisms of gait and probably reinforce hyperextension. But independence and safety are important considerations. The therapist can facilitate a normal gait pattern in therapy and incorporate it into adaptive gait as much as possible. If pushing a rollator encourages stiff knees and trunk, lower extremity equilibrium and trunk elongation can be emphasized. Wearing a unilateral orthotic may require extra attention to weight shifting over the involved side.

Behaviors involving upper extremity prostheses and lower extremity orthoses or prostheses are included at the end of this section.

Demonstration of Independent Locomotion with Normal Movement Patterns

Behaviors	Conditions	Measurements
The student will 1. kick with legs to move body short distances in supine 2. roll to locomote short distances 3. roll segmentally to locomote short distances 4. scoot body in sitting to locomote short distances 5. assume the prone position in preparation for locomotion 6. hitch with arms in prone 7. prone crawl reciprocally 8. demonstrate left-right symmetry in prone crawling 9. grade reciprocal prone crawling 10. assume quadruped in preparation for locomotion 11. come to quadruped from sidesitting in preparation for locomotion 12. creep reciprocally in quadruped 13. creep backwards reciprocally in quadruped	A. with maximum–moderate assistance B. with moderate–minimum assistance C. with __% assistance D. with guarding assistance E. with facilitation F. with tactile cues G. with proprioceptive cues H. with a demonstration I. with verbal cues J. in the therapy setting K. independently L. in functional activities	a. 1 out of 4 times b. 2 out of 4 times c. 3 out of 4 times d. 4 out of 4 times e. __% of the time f. in/for 0–5 seconds g. in/for 5–30 seconds h. in/for 30–60 seconds i. in/for over 1 minute j. in/for __ minutes k. 1 repetition l. 2–5 repetitions m. 6–10 repetitions n. over 10 repetitions o. __ repetitions p. 0–5 feet q. 5–15 feet r. 15–25 feet s. over 25 feet t. __ feet u. to/at mid range/level v. to/at functional range/level w. to/at normal limits x. to/at __% of normal y. to/at __ degrees

Demonstration of Independent Locomotion with Normal Movement Patterns continued

Behaviors	Conditions	Measurements
14. demonstrate left-right symmetry in creeping	A. with maximum–moderate assistance	a. 1 out of 4 times
15. creep with proper weightbearing alignment of extremities	B. with moderate–minimum assistance	b. 2 out of 4 times
16. creep with weight on ulnar palm and with fingers extended	C. with __% assistance	c. 3 out of 4 times
17. creep with pelvis in neutral	D. with guarding assistance	d. 4 out of 4 times
18. creep with elongation on the weightbearing side	E. with facilitation	e. __% of the time
19. grade reciprocal creeping	F. with tactile cues	f. in/for 0–5 seconds
20. assume a kneeling position in preparation for locomotion	G. with proprioceptive cues	g. in/for 5–30 seconds
21. kneel walk	H. with a demonstration	h. in/for 30–60 seconds
22. kneel walk with left-right symmetry	I. with verbal cues	i. in/for over 1 minute
23. kneel walk with head and trunk in neutral	J. in the therapy setting	j. in/for __ minutes
24. kneel walk with pelvis in neutral	K. independently	k. 1 repetition
25. kneel walk with reciprocal arm swing	L. in functional activities	l. 2–5 repetitions
26. kneel walk with elongation on the weightbearing side		m. 6–10 repetitions
27. grade kneel walking		n. over 10 repetitions
		o. __ repetitions
		p. 0–5 feet
		q. 5–15 feet
		r. 15–25 feet
		s. over 25 feet
		t. __ feet
		u. to/at mid range/level
		v. to/at functional range/level
		w. to/at normal limits
		x. to/at __% of normal
		y. to/at __ degrees

Walking Independently with Normal Gait Pattern and Graded Control

Behaviors	Conditions	Measurements
The student will 28. rise to standing from a seated position 29. keep weight forward in standing from a seated position 30. rise from a seated position with graded control 31. seat self in chair from a standing position 32. locate chair with legs before sitting from a standing position 33. reach back for armrest(s) before sitting from a standing position 34. seat self in chair from a standing position with graded control 35. pull or push up to a standing position 36. pull or push to standing position through half-kneeling 37. pull or push to standing position without hyperextension thrust 38. stand at and cruise along a supporting surface 39. cruise along a supporting surface with weight forward	A. with maximum–moderate assistance B. with moderate–minimum assistance C. with __% assistance D. with guarding assistance E. with facilitation F. with tactile cues G. with proprioceptive cues H. with a demonstration I. with verbal cues J. in the therapy setting K. independently L. in functional activities	a. 1 out of 4 times b. 2 out of 4 times c. 3 out of 4 times d. 4 out of 4 times e. __% of the time f. in/for 0–5 seconds g. in/for 5–30 seconds h. in/for 30–60 seconds i. in/for over 1 minute j. in/for __ minutes k. 1 repetition l. 2–5 repetitions m. 6–10 repetitions n. over 10 repetitions o. __ repetitions p. 0–5 feet q. 5–15 feet r. 15–25 feet s. over 25 feet t. __ feet u. to/at mid range/level v. to/at functional range/level w. to/at normal limits x. to/at __% of normal y. to/at __ degrees

Walking Independently with Normal Gait Pattern and Graded Control continued

Behaviors	Conditions	Measurements
40. come to standing from the floor through half-kneeling 41. keep weight forward in coming to stand through half-kneeling 42. come to stand through half-kneeling with graded control 43. get to the floor from a standing position 44. get to the floor from a standing position with graded control 45. get to the floor from a standing position using trunk flexion-rotation and upper extremity weightbearing 46. eliminate scissoring in gait 47. walk 48. walk with equal length of strides 49. walk with equal timing of strides 50. walk with symmetrical weight shifts 51. walk with a reciprocal symmetrical arm swing 52. walk with a symmetrical gait pattern 53. demonstrate a heel-toe gait pattern	A. with maximum–moderate assistance B. with moderate–minimum assistance C. with __% assistance D. with guarding assistance E. with facilitation F. with tactile cues G. with proprioceptive cues H. with a demonstration I. with verbal cues J. in the therapy setting K. independently L. in functional activities	a. 1 out of 4 times b. 2 out of 4 times c. 3 out of 4 times d. 4 out of 4 times e. __% of the time f. in/for 0–5 seconds g. in/for 5–30 seconds h. in/for 30–60 seconds i. in/for over 1 minute j. in/for __ minutes k. 1 repetition l. 2–5 repetitions m. 6–10 repetitions n. over 10 repetitions o. __ repetitions p. 0–5 feet q. 5–15 feet r. 15–25 feet s. over 25 feet t. __ feet u. to/at mid range/level v. to/at functional range/level w. to/at normal limits x. to/at __% of normal y. to/at __ degrees

Walking Independently with Normal Gait Pattern and Graded Control continued

Behaviors	Conditions	Measurements
54. bear weight on the lateral borders of the feet in gait	A. with maximum–moderate assistance	a. 1 out of 4 times
	B. with moderate–minimum assistance	b. 2 out of 4 times
55. demonstrate an appropriate pushoff, midswing, heel-strike, and midstance in gait	C. with __% assistance	c. 3 out of 4 times
	D. with guarding assistance	d. 4 out of 4 times
56. walk with weight slightly forward	E. with facilitation	e. __% of the time
57. walk with trunk rotation toward the nonweightbearing side	F. with tactile cues	f. in/for 0–5 seconds
	G. with proprioceptive cues	g. in/for 5–30 seconds
58. walk with elongation on the weightbearing side	H. with a demonstration	h. in/for 30–60 seconds
	I. with verbal cues	i. in/for over 1 minute
59. walk with slight hip external rotation on the nonweightbearing side	J. in the therapy setting	j. in/for __ minutes
	K. independently	k. 1 repetition
60. demonstrate all the components of equilibrium in gait	L. in functional activities	l. 2–5 repetitions
		m. 6–10 repetitions
61. walk with the pelvis in neutral		n. over 10 repetitions
		o. __ repetitions
62. maintain head, shoulders, trunk, and pelvis in alignment over the base of support in gait		p. 0–5 feet
		q. 5–15 feet
		r. 15–25 feet
63. maintain the arm(s) in a position of reduced hypertonic posturing in gait		s. over 25 feet
		t. __ feet
		u. to/at mid range/level
64. walk with graded control		v. to/at functional range/level
65. walk sidewards		w. to/at normal limits
		x. to/at __% of normal
		y. to/at __ degrees

Walking Independently with Normal Gait Pattern and Graded Control continued

Behaviors	Conditions	Measurements
66. walk sidewards with proper postural alignment	A. with maximum–moderate assistance	a. 1 out of 4 times
67. walk sidewards with graded control	B. with moderate–minimum assistance	b. 2 out of 4 times
68. walk backwards	C. with __% assistance	c. 3 out of 4 times
69. walk backwards with proper postural alignment	D. with guarding assistance	d. 4 out of 4 times
70. walk backwards with graded control	E. with facilitation	e. __% of the time
71. develop the endurance for functional gait in the classroom	F. with tactile cues	f. in/for 0–5 seconds
72. develop the speed and endurance for functional gait in the school building	G. with proprioceptive cues	g. in/for 5–30 seconds
73. develop the speed and endurance for functional gait on the playground	H. with a demonstration	h. in/for 30–60 seconds
74. demonstrate sufficient balance and awareness of safety to walk without supervision	I. with verbal cues	i. in/for over 1 minute
75. demonstrate the ability to fall safely	J. in the therapy setting	j. in/for __ minutes
76. walk on uneven surfaces	K. independently	k. 1 repetition
77. walk up a ramp	L. in functional activities	l. 2–5 repetitions
78. walk down a ramp		m. 6–10 repetitions
79. climb stairs with one hand held		n. over 10 repetitions
80. descend stairs with one hand held		o. __ repetitions
		p. 0–5 feet
		q. 5–15 feet
		r. 15–25 feet
		s. over 25 feet
		t. __ feet
		u. to/at mid range/level
		v. to/at functional range/level
		w. to/at normal limits
		x. to/at __% of normal
		y. to/at __ degrees

Walking Independently with Normal Gait Pattern and Graded Control continued

Behaviors	Conditions	Measurements
81. climb stairs using a railing	A. with maximum–moderate assistance	a. 1 out of 4 times
82. descend stairs using a railing	B. with moderate–minimum assistance	b. 2 out of 4 times
83. use stairs with a railing with proper postural alignment and graded control	C. with __% assistance	c. 3 out of 4 times
84. climb stairs without a railing	D. with guarding assistance	d. 4 out of 4 times
85. descend stairs without a railing	E. with facilitation	e. __% of the time
86. use stairs without a railing with proper postural alignment and graded control	F. with tactile cues	f. in/for 0–5 seconds
87. run	G. with proprioceptive cues	g. in/for 5–30 seconds
88. demonstrate sufficient control to run without falling	H. with a demonstration	h. in/for 30–60 seconds
89. run with weight forward and arms pumping	I. with verbal cues	i. in/for over 1 minute
90. run with a symmetrical pattern	J. in the therapy setting	j. in/for __ minutes
91. run with elongation on the weightbearing side	K. independently	k. 1 repetition
92. run with graded control	L. in functional activities	l. 2–5 repetitions
93. control stopping while running		m. 6–10 repetitions
		n. over 10 repetitions
		o. __ repetitions
		p. 0–5 feet
		q. 5–15 feet
		r. 15–25 feet
		s. over 25 feet
		t. __ feet
		u. to/at mid range/level
		v. to/at functional range/level
		w. to/at normal limits
		x. to/at __% of normal
		y. to/at __ degrees

Demonstration of Appropriate Use of Adaptive Equipment

Behaviors	Conditions	Measurements
The student will 94. locomote with a scooter board 95. locomote with a crawligator 96. weight-bear with proper postural alignment in a standing box 97. walk in a ring walker with a seat 98. walk in a ring walker without a seat 99. walk with head and trunk in neutral in a ring walker 100. keep weight forward and legs in proper weightbearing position in a ring walker 101. walk in a ring walker with a reciprocal gait 102. walk in parallel bars 103. walk in parallel bars with weight forward 104. walk in parallel bars with a symmetrical gait 105. walk in parallel bars with legs in proper weightbearing position 106. walk in parallel bars with graded control 107. turn around in parallel bars 108. walk with a rollator	A. with maximum–moderate assistance B. with moderate–minimum assistance C. with __% assistance D. with guarding assistance E. with facilitation F. with tactile cues G. with proprioceptive cues H. with a demonstration I. with verbal cues J. in the therapy setting K. independently L. in functional activities	a. 1 out of 4 times b. 2 out of 4 times c. 3 out of 4 times d. 4 out of 4 times e. __% of the time f. in/for 0–5 seconds g. in/for 5–30 seconds h. in/for 30–60 seconds i. in/for over 1 minute j. in/for __ minutes k. 1 repetition l. 2–5 repetitions m. 6–10 repetitions n. over 10 repetitions o. __ repetitions p. 0–5 feet q. 5–15 feet r. 15–25 feet s. over 25 feet t. __ feet u. to/at mid range/level v. to/at functional range/level w. to/at normal limits x. to/at __% of normal y. to/at __ degrees

IV Locomotion and Gait

Demonstration of Appropriate Use of Adaptive Equipment continued

Behaviors	Conditions	Measurements
109. walk with a geriatric walker	A. with maximum–moderate assistance	a. 1 out of 4 times
110. walk with a reciprocal walker		b. 2 out of 4 times
111. walk with axillary crutch(es)	B. with moderate–minimum assistance	c. 3 out of 4 times
112. walk with Lofstrand crutch(es)	C. with __% assistance	d. 4 out of 4 times
113. walk with quad cane(s)	D. with guarding assistance	e. __% of the time
114. walk with straight cane(s)	E. with facilitation	f. in/for 0–5 seconds
115. use proper hand grip with assistive devices	F. with tactile cues	g. in/for 5–30 seconds
116. use assistive devices with legs in proper weightbearing position	G. with proprioceptive cues	h. in/for 30–60 seconds
117. keep weight slightly forward while using assistive devices	H. with a demonstration	i. in/for over 1 minute
118. use appropriate gait pattern with assistive devices	I. with verbal cues	j. in/for __ minutes
119. demonstrate a symmetrical gait pattern with assistive devices	J. in the therapy setting	k. 1 repetition
120. show ___ components of equilibrium in walking with assistive devices	K. independently	l. 2–5 repetitions
121. use assistive devices with graded control	L. in functional activities	m. 6–10 repetitions
122. stand up and resume sitting with correct placement of assistive devices		n. over 10 repetitions
		o. __ repetitions
		p. 0–5 feet
		q. 5–15 feet
		r. 15–25 feet
		s. over 25 feet
		t. __ feet
		u. to/at mid range/level
		v. to/at functional range/level
		w. to/at normal limits
		x. to/at __% of normal
		y. to/at __ degrees

Demonstration of Appropriate Use of Adaptive Equipment continued

Behaviors	Conditions	Measurements
123. walk on uneven terrain with assistive devices	A. with maximum–moderate assistance	a. 1 out of 4 times
		b. 2 out of 4 times
124. climb a ramp with assistive devices	B. with moderate–minimum assistance	c. 3 out of 4 times
		d. 4 out of 4 times
125. descend a ramp with assistive devices	C. with __% assistance	e. __% of the time
126. climb stairs with assistive devices	D. with guarding assistance	f. in/for 0–5 seconds
127. descend stairs with assistive devices		g. in/for 5–30 seconds
	E. with facilitation	h. in/for 30–60 seconds
128. use proper gait pattern on stairs with assistive devices	F. with tactile cues	i. in/for over 1 minute
	G. with proprioceptive cues	j. in/for __ minutes
129. use stairs with assistive devices with graded control		k. 1 repetition
	H. with a demonstration	l. 2–5 repetitions
130. demonstrate appropriate safety techniques in the use of assistive devices	I. with verbal cues	m. 6–10 repetitions
	J. in the therapy setting	n. over 10 repetitions
	K. independently	o. __ repetitions
131. fall safely while using assistive devices	L. in functional activities	p. 0–5 feet
132. stand up from the floor with assistive devices		q. 5–15 feet
		r. 15–25 feet
133. advance from a nonweightbearing to a partial-weightbearing gait		s. over 25 feet
		t. __ feet
134. advance from a partial-weightbearing to a full-weightbearing gait		u. to/at mid range/level
		v. to/at functional range/level
135. advance from a 4-point to a 2-point gait		w. to/at normal limits
		x. to/at __% of normal
136. advance to ambulation without assistive devices		y. to/at __ degrees

Demonstration of Functional Independence in the Use of Orthoses or Prostheses

Behaviors	Conditions	Measurements
The student will		
137. stabilize shoulder girdle to use upper extremity prosthesis (or prostheses)	A. with maximum–moderate assistance	a. 1 out of 4 times
		b. 2 out of 4 times
138. dissociate proximal from distal arm movements in the use of upper extremity prosthesis (or prostheses)	B. with moderate–minimum assistance	c. 3 out of 4 times
	C. with __% assistance	d. 4 out of 4 times
	D. with guarding assistance	e. __% of the time
139. demonstrate isolated movements of an upper extremity prosthesis	E. with facilitation	f. in/for 0–5 seconds
	F. with tactile cues	g. in/for 5–30 seconds
		h. in/for 30–60 seconds
140. demonstrate a ____ movement of an upper extremity prosthesis	G. with proprioceptive cues	i. in/for over 1 minute
		j. in/for __ minutes
	H. with a demonstration	k. 1 repetition
141. use an upper extremity prosthesis as an assist	I. with verbal cues	l. 2–5 repetitions
	J. in the therapy setting	m. 6–10 repetitions
142. use an upper extremity prosthesis in bilateral motor activities	K. independently	n. over 10 repetitions
	L. in functional activities	o. __ repetitions
		p. 0–5 feet
143. demonstrate isolated movements of bilateral upper extremity prostheses		q. 5–15 feet
		r. 15–25 feet
		s. over 25 feet
144. demonstrate a ____ movement of the dominant upper extremity prosthesis		t. __ feet
		u. to/at mid range/level
145. demonstrate a ____ movement of the nondominant upper extremity prosthesis		v. to/at functional range/level
		w. to/at normal limits
146. use upper extremity prostheses in bilateral gross motor activities		x. to/at __% of normal
		y. to/at __ degrees

Demonstration of Functional Independence in the Use of Orthoses or Prostheses continued

Behaviors	Conditions	Measurements
147. use upper extremity prostheses in ADL	A. with maximum–moderate assistance	a. 1 out of 4 times
148. use upper extremity prostheses in bilateral fine motor activities	B. with moderate–minimum assistance	b. 2 out of 4 times
		c. 3 out of 4 times
	C. with __% assistance	d. 4 out of 4 times
149. put on and take off upper extremity prostheses	D. with guarding assistance	e. __% of the time
		f. in/for 0–5 seconds
150. show appropriate use of upper extremity splints	E. with facilitation	g. in/for 5–30 seconds
	F. with tactile cues	h. in/for 30–60 seconds
151. put on and take off upper extremity splints	G. with proprioceptive cues	i. in/for over 1 minute
		j. in/for __ minutes
152. demonstrate proper body alignment with the use of lower extremity braces or prostheses	H. with a demonstration	k. 1 repetition
	I. with verbal cues	l. 2–5 repetitions
	J. in the therapy setting	m. 6–10 repetitions
	K. independently	n. over 10 repetitions
153. use appropriate gait pattern with lower extremity braces or prostheses	L. in functional activities	o. __ repetitions
		p. 0–5 feet
154. use symmetrical gait pattern with lower extremity braces or prostheses		q. 5–15 feet
		r. 15–25 feet
		s. over 25 feet
155. walk with lower extremity braces or prostheses with graded control		t. __ feet
		u. to/at mid range/level
156. demonstrate appropriate safety techniques in the use of lower extremity braces or prostheses		v. to/at functional range/level
		w. to/at normal limits
		x. to/at __% of normal
157. walk on uneven terrain with lower extremity braces or prostheses		y. to/at __ degrees

Demonstration of Functional Independence in the Use of Orthoses or Prostheses continued

Behaviors	Conditions	Measurements
158. climb a ramp with lower extremity braces or prostheses 159. descend a ramp with lower extremity braces or prostheses 160. climb stairs with lower extremity braces or prostheses 161. descend stairs with lower extremity braces or prostheses 162. remove braces or prostheses 163. put on braces or prostheses 164. lock and unlock long leg braces	A. with maximum–moderate assistance B. with moderate–minimum assistance C. with __% assistance D. with guarding assistance E. with facilitation F. with tactile cues G. with proprioceptive cues H. with a demonstration I. with verbal cues J. in the therapy setting K. independently L. in functional activities	a. 1 out of 4 times b. 2 out of 4 times c. 3 out of 4 times d. 4 out of 4 times e. __% of the time f. in/for 0–5 seconds g. in/for 5–30 seconds h. in/for 30–60 seconds i. in/for over 1 minute j. in/for __ minutes k. 1 repetition l. 2–5 repetitions m. 6–10 repetitions n. over 10 repetitions o. __ repetitions p. 0–5 feet q. 5–15 feet r. 15–25 feet s. over 25 feet t. __ feet u. to/at mid range/level v. to/at functional range/level w. to/at normal limits x. to/at __% of normal y. to/at __ degrees

Additional Objectives

Behaviors	Conditions	Measurements
The student will 165.	A. with maximum–moderate assistance B. with moderate–minimum assistance C. with __% assistance D. with guarding assistance E. with facilitation F. with tactile cues G. with proprioceptive cues H. with a demonstration I. with verbal cues J. in the therapy setting K. independently L. in functional activities	a. 1 out of 4 times b. 2 out of 4 times c. 3 out of 4 times d. 4 out of 4 times e. __% of the time f. in/for 0–5 seconds g. in/for 5–30 seconds h. in/for 30–60 seconds i. in/for over 1 minute j. in/for __ minutes k. 1 repetition l. 2–5 repetitions m. 6–10 repetitions n. over 10 repetitions o. __ repetitions p. 0–5 feet q. 5–15 feet r. 15–25 feet s. over 25 feet t. __ feet u. to/at mid range/level v. to/at functional range/level w. to/at normal limits x. to/at __% of normal y. to/at __ degrees

Wheelchair Skills V

Normal movement components play a big role in the functional use of a wheelchair and are essential for safety in transfers. Most of the work that will lead to wheelchair independence is done when addressing tone, proximal stability, and equilibrium. For example, in order to more effectively "propel the wheelchair with bilateral arm movements" (V-6), the student may need to "dissociate head from body movements" (I-44), "maintain shoulder girdle stability to grade upper extremity movement" (III-55), and "bring head, shoulders, and trunk into alignment over the base of support in sitting" (III-204). In order to "perform transfers between the wheelchair and the floor" (V-29), the student may need to "support body weight with arm to prevent falling" (III-45), "maintain upper extremity weightbearing with trunk rotation" (III-31), and "move body over weightbearing arm" (III-32).

Demonstration of Functional Independence in the Use of a Wheelchair

Behaviors	*Conditions*	*Measurements*
The student will		
1. sit in a wheelchair with proper postural alignment	A. with maximum–moderate assistance	a. 1 out of 4 times
		b. 2 out of 4 times
2. propel wheelchair with proper postural alignment	B. with moderate–minimum assistance	c. 3 out of 4 times
		d. 4 out of 4 times
	C. with __% assistance	e. __% of the time
3. use wheelchair accessories appropriately	D. with guarding assistance	f. in/for 0–5 seconds
		g. in/for 5–30 seconds
4. lock and unlock wheelchair	E. with facilitation	h. in/for 30–60 seconds
5. propel the wheelchair forward	F. with tactile cues	i. in/for over 1 minute
	G. with proprioceptive cues	j. in/for __ minutes
6. propel the wheelchair with bilateral arm movements		k. 1 repetition
	H. with a demonstration	l. 2–5 repetitions
7. dissociate arms from head and trunk to propel wheelchair	I. with verbal cues	m. 6–10 repetitions
	J. in the therapy setting	n. over 10 repetitions
	K. independently	o. __ repetitions
8. propel a one-arm-drive wheelchair	L. in functional activities	p. 0–5 feet
9. propel the wheelchair in various directions		q. 5–15 feet
		r. 15–25 feet
10. propel the wheelchair accurately in the desired direction		s. over 25 feet
		t. __ feet
11. maneuver the wheelchair accurately through narrow spaces		u. to/at mid range/level
		v. to/at functional range/level
12. respond quickly to stop the wheelchair		w. to/at normal limits
		x. to/at __% of normal
		y. to/at __ degrees

Demonstration of Functional Independence in the Use of a Wheelchair continued

Behaviors	Conditions	Measurements
13. propel the wheelchair with functional speed 14. safely ascend and descend a ramp in the wheelchair 15. propel the wheelchair on uneven terrain 16. develop the endurance and control to propel the wheelchair within the classroom 17. develop the endurance and control to propel the wheelchair in a variety of school activities 18. develop the endurance and control in wheelchair locomotion to use various public facilities 19. demonstrate sufficient control and awareness of safety to use a wheelchair without supervision	A. with maximum–moderate assistance B. with moderate–minimum assistance C. with __% assistance D. with guarding assistance E. with facilitation F. with tactile cues G. with proprioceptive cues H. with a demonstration I. with verbal cues J. in the therapy setting K. independently L. in functional activities	a. 1 out of 4 times b. 2 out of 4 times c. 3 out of 4 times d. 4 out of 4 times e. __% of the time f. in/for 0–5 seconds g. in/for 5–30 seconds h. in/for 30–60 seconds i. in/for over 1 minute j. in/for __ minutes k. 1 repetition l. 2–5 repetitions m. 6–10 repetitions n. over 10 repetitions o. __ repetitions p. 0–5 feet q. 5–15 feet r. 15–25 feet s. over 25 feet t. __ feet u. to/at mid range/level v. to/at functional range/level w. to/at normal limits x. to/at __% of normal y. to/at __ degrees

Development of Functional Independence in Wheelchair Transfers

Behaviors	*Conditions*	*Measurements*
The student will		
20. align the wheelchair and observe safety procedures for transfers	A. with maximum–moderate assistance	a. 1 out of 4 times
		b. 2 out of 4 times
21. dissociate arms from rest of body for reaching in wheelchair transfers	B. with moderate–minimum assistance	c. 3 out of 4 times
		d. 4 out of 4 times
	C. with __% assistance	e. __% of the time
22. dissociate left from right arm for wheelchair transfers	D. with guarding assistance	f. in/for 0.5 seconds
		g. in/for 5–30 seconds
	E. with facilitation	h. in/for 30–60 seconds
23. perform transfers between the wheelchair and a regular chair	F. with tactile cues	i. in/for over 1 minute
	G. with proprioceptive cues	j. in/for __ minutes
24. remove arm rest and position sliding board for sliding transfers		k. 1 repetition
	H. with a demonstration	l. 2–5 repetitions
	I. with verbal cues	m. 6–10 repetitions
25. perform transfers between the wheelchair and a standing position at a urinal	J. in the therapy setting	n. over 10 repetitions
	K. independently	o. __ repetitions
	L. in functional activities	p. 0–5 feet
26. adjust clothing in wheelchair in order to use a urinal		q. 5–15 feet
		r. 15–25 feet
27. perform transfers between the wheelchair and a toilet		s. over 25 feet
		t. __ feet
28. adjust clothing in wheelchair in order to use a toilet		u. to/at mid range/level
		v. to/at functional range/level
29. perform transfers between the wheelchair and the floor		w. to/at normal limits
		x. to/at __% of normal
		y. to/at __ degrees

Development of Functional Independence in Wheelchair Transfers continued

Behaviors	Conditions	Measurements
30. use flexion-rotation and upper extremity weightbearing in wheelchair-to-floor transfers 31. grade lowering self to the floor from the wheelchair 32. transfer from the floor to the wheelchair through half-kneeling 33. perform transfers between the wheelchair and a bed 34. perform transfers between the wheelchair and a bathtub 35. perform transfers between the wheelchair and a car 36. perform wheelchair transfers with graded control 37. demonstrate sufficient control and awareness of safety to perform wheelchair transfers without supervision	A. with maximum–moderate assistance B. with moderate–minimum assistance C. with __% assistance D. with guarding assistance E. with facilitation F. with tactile cues G. with proprioceptive cues H. with a demonstration I. with verbal cues J. in the therapy setting K. independently L. in functional activities	a. 1 out of 4 times b. 2 out of 4 times c. 3 out of 4 times d. 4 out of 4 times e. __% of the time f. in/for 0–5 seconds g. in/for 5–30 seconds h. in/for 30–60 seconds i. in/for over 1 minute j. in/for __ minutes k. 1 repetition l. 2–5 repetitions m. 6–10 repetitions n. over 10 repetitions o. __ repetitions p. 0–5 feet q. 5–15 feet r. 15–25 feet s. over 25 feet t. __ feet u. to/at mid range/level v. to/at functional range/level w. to/at normal limits x. to/at __% of normal y. to/at __ degrees

Additional Objectives

Behaviors	Conditions	Measurements
The student will		
38	A. with maximum–moderate assistance	a. 1 out of 4 times
	B. with moderate–minimum assistance	b. 2 out of 4 times
	C. with __% assistance	c. 3 out of 4 times
	D. with guarding assistance	d. 4 out of 4 times
	E. with facilitation	e. __% of the time
	F. with tactile cues	f. in/for 0–5 seconds
	G. with proprioceptive cues	g. in/for 5–30 seconds
	H. with a demonstration	h. in/for 30–60 seconds
	I. with verbal cues	i. in/for over 1 minute
	J. in the therapy setting	j. in/for __ minutes
	K. independently	k. 1 repetition
	L. in functional activities	l. 2–5 repetitions
		m. 6–10 repetitions
		n. over 10 repetitions
		o. __ repetitions
		p. 0–5 feet
		q. 5–15 feet
		r. 15–25 feet
		s. over 25 feet
		t. __ feet
		u. to/at mid range/level
		v. to/at functional range/level
		w. to/at normal limits
		x. to/at __% of normal
		y. to/at __ degrees

Exercise (ROM, Strength, and Endurance)   VI

Improving range of motion, strength, and endurance are very common goals for children with a variety of disabilities. These goals are often seen on doctors' orders, are more easily measured than those in the first three sections, and are easily understood by nontherapists. With orthopedic, neuromuscular, and even developmental disabilities, there are times when the focus of therapy is on specific body parts instead of movement patterns. One major concern, among others, may be to build up the quadriceps prior to knee surgery, to attack a lordosis through abdominal strengthening, or to isolate hip extension so a child can take a step backwards to the wheelchair. As preferable as active range of motion is, some severely handicapped children must be passively ranged.

Cardiopulmonary capacity and bowel and bladder control are compromised with many handicapped children. These areas are addressed under the last goal listed in this section.

Increase of Joint Range of Motion to within Normal Limits

Behaviors	Conditions	Measurements
The student will 1. tolerate positioning in adaptive equipment 2. tolerate splinting 3. tolerate passive range of motion 4. tolerate range of motion with stretch 5. actively perform stretching of tight muscles 6. perform self-ranging to hemiparetic side 7. maintain joint range of motion 8. increase range of motion at specific joints 9. increase range of motion at the _____ joint(s) 10. increase range of motion at the _____ joint(s) to _____ degrees of _____ 11. increase range of motion of the hemiparetic side 12. increase neck mobility 13. increase range of neck extensors to allow chin tuck 14. increase range of neck musculature to allow symmetry in head control 15. increase trunk mobility 16. increase trunk rotation	A. with maximum–moderate assistance B. with moderate–minimum assistance C. with __% assistance D. with guarding assistance E. with facilitation F. with tactile cues G. with proprioceptive cues H. with a demonstration I. with verbal cues J. in the therapy setting K. independently L. in functional activities	a. 1 out of 4 times b. 2 out of 4 times c. 3 out of 4 times d. 4 out of 4 times e. __% of the time f. in/for 0–5 seconds g. in/for 5–30 seconds h. in/for 30–60 seconds i. in/for over 1 minute j. in/for __ minutes k. 1 repetition l. 2–5 repetitions m. 6–10 repetitions n. over 10 repetitions o. __ repetitions p. 0–5 feet q. 5–15 feet r. 15–25 feet s. over 25 feet t. __ feet u. to/at mid range/level v. to/at functional range/level w. to/at normal limits x. to/at __% of normal y. to/at __ degrees

Increase of Joint Range of Motion to within Normal Limits continued

Behaviors	*Conditions*	*Measurements*
17. increase range of trunk musculature to allow symmetry in trunk control	A. with maximum–moderate assistance	a. 1 out of 4 times
18. increase range of trunk musculature to reduce kyphosis	B. with moderate–minimum assistance	b. 2 out of 4 times
19. increase range of trunk musculature to reduce lordosis	C. with ___% assistance	c. 3 out of 4 times
20. increase range of trunk musculature to reduce scoliosis	D. with guarding assistance	d. 4 out of 4 times
21. increase shoulder girdle mobility	E. with facilitation	e. ___% of the time
22. reduce scapulohumeral tightness to allow sidelying with arm overhead	F. with tactile cues	f. in/for 0–5 seconds
23. increase range of shoulder girdle to allow sufficient mobility for ADL	G. with proprioceptive cues	g. in/for 5–30 seconds
24. increase range of upper extremity joints to allow for properly aligned weightbearing	H. with a demonstration	h. in/for 30–60 seconds
25. increase range of upper extremity joints to perform fine motor activities	I. with verbal cues	i. in/for over 1 minute
26. increase range in supination to allow opposition of palms	J. in the therapy setting	j. in/for ___ minutes
27. increase pelvic mobility	K. independently	k. 1 repetition
28. increase low back range to allow a posterior pelvic tilt	L. in functional activities	l. 2–5 repetitions
		m. 6–10 repetitions
		n. over 10 repetitions
		o. ___ repetitions
		p. 0–5 feet
		q. 5–15 feet
		r. 15–25 feet
		s. over 25 feet
		t. ___ feet
		u. to/at mid range/level
		v. to/at functional range/level
		w. to/at normal limits
		x. to/at ___% of normal
		y. to/at ___ degrees

Increase of Joint Range of Motion to within Normal Limits continued

Behaviors	Conditions	Measurements
29. increase range at shoulders and hips to assume a full prone position with arms overhead 30. increase range at hips to allow bolster sitting 31. increase range at hips to allow tailor sitting 32. increase range at hips to allow sidesitting 33. increase range of hamstrings to allow longsitting 34. increase range at hips to eliminate scissoring 35. increase range of lower extremity joints to allow properly aligned weightbearing	A. with maximum–moderate assistance B. with moderate–minimum assistance C. with __% assistance D. with guarding assistance E. with facilitation F. with tactile cues G. with proprioceptive cues H. with a demonstration I. with verbal cues J. in the therapy setting K. independently L. in functional activities	a. 1 out of 4 times b. 2 out of 4 times c. 3 out of 4 times d. 4 out of 4 times e. __% of the time f. in/for 0–5 seconds g. in/for 5–30 seconds h. in/for 30–60 seconds i. in/for over 1 minute j. in/for __ minutes k. 1 repetition l. 2–5 repetitions m. 6–10 repetitions n. over 10 repetitions o. __ repetitions p. 0–5 feet q. 5–15 feet r. 15–25 feet s. over 25 feet t. __ feet u. to/at mid range/level v. to/at functional range/level w. to/at normal limits x. to/at __% of normal y. to/at __ degrees

Increase of Muscle Strength and Endurance to within Normal Limits

Behaviors	Conditions	Measurements
The student will		
36. contract a specific muscle or muscle group	A. with maximum–moderate assistance	a. 1 out of 4 times
37. maintain the contraction of a specific muscle or muscle group	B. with moderate–minimum assistance	b. 2 out of 4 times
38. isolate movements of flexion-extension	C. with __% assistance	c. 3 out of 4 times
39. isolate movements of abduction-adduction-lateral flexion	D. with guarding assistance	d. 4 out of 4 times
40. isolate movements of rotation	E. with facilitation	e. __% of the time
41. isolate movements of _____ at the _____ joint(s)	F. with tactile cues	f. in/for 0–5 seconds
42. isolate thumb-finger movements	G. with proprioceptive cues	g. in/for 5–30 seconds
43. perform the movement(s) of _____ through partial range	H. with a demonstration	h. in/for 30–60 seconds
44. perform the movement(s) of _____ through full range	I. with verbal cues	i. in/for over 1 minute
45. perform the movement(s) of _____ against gravity	J. in the therapy setting	j. in/for __ minutes
46. perform the movement(s) of _____ against manual resistance	K. independently	k. 1 repetition
47. increase muscle strength to the _____ level (P, F, G, N)	L. in functional activities	l. 2–5 repetitions
48. increase strength of the _____ muscle(s) to the _____ level (P, F, G, N)		m. 6–10 repetitions
		n. over 10 repetitions
		o. __ repetitions
		p. 0–5 feet
		q. 5–15 feet
		r. 15–25 feet
		s. over 25 feet
		t. __ feet
		u. to/at mid range/level
		v. to/at functional range/level
		w. to/at normal limits
		x. to/at __% of normal
		y. to/at __ degrees

Increase of Muscle Strength and Endurance to within Normal Limits continued

Behaviors	Conditions	Measurements
49. maintain overall muscle strength and endurance	A. with maximum–moderate assistance	a. 1 out of 4 times
50. increase overall muscle strength and endurance	B. with moderate–minimum assistance	b. 2 out of 4 times
51. perform diagonal patterns of movement	C. with __% assistance	c. 3 out of 4 times
52. take resistance in diagonal patterns of movement	D. with guarding assistance	d. 4 out of 4 times
53. increase strength and endurance of the hemiparetic side	E. with facilitation	e. __% of the time
54. increase strength and endurance of neck musculature for sustained head control	F. with tactile cues	f. in/for 0–5 seconds
55. maintain the head in neutral with manual resistance	G. with proprioceptive cues	g. in/for 5–30 seconds
56. adjust and maintain posture so shoulders are level	H. with a demonstration	h. in/for 30–60 seconds
57. adjust and maintain posture so pelvis is level	I. with verbal cues	i. in/for over 1 minute
58. increase trunk symmetry in range and strength to reduce scoliotic curve	J. in the therapy setting	j. in/for __ minutes
59. increase strength and endurance of trunk musculature	K. independently	k. 1 repetition
60. maintain the trunk in neutral with manual resistance	L. in functional activities	l. 2–5 repetitions
		m. 6–10 repetitions
		n. over 10 repetitions
		o. __ repetitions
		p. 0–5 feet
		q. 5–15 feet
		r. 15–25 feet
		s. over 25 feet
		t. __ feet
		u. to/at mid range/level
		v. to/at functional range/level
		w. to/at normal limits
		x. to/at __% of normal
		y. to/at __ degrees

Increase of Muscle Strength and Endurance to within Normal Limits continued

Behaviors	Conditions	Measurements
61. increase abdominal strength 62. perform a posterior pelvic tilt 63. increase proximal strength and endurance to maintain aligned antigravity postures 64. increase upper extremity strength and endurance 65. maintain the upper extremity joints as positioned with manual resistance 66. increase upper extremity strength to allow for sustained weightbearing 67. increase upper extremity strength for performance of fine motor activities 68. hypertrophy upper extremity musculature to compensate for lower extremity weakness or paralysis 69. increase lower extremity strength and endurance 70. maintain the lower extremity joints as positioned with manual resistance 71. increase lower extremity strength to allow for sustained weightbearing 72. develop the strength to perform functional activities in the classroom	A. with maximum–moderate assistance B. with moderate–minimum assistance C. with __% assistance D. with guarding assistance E. with facilitation F. with tactile cues G. with proprioceptive cues H. with a demonstration I. with verbal cues J. in the therapy setting K. independently L. in functional activities	a. 1 out of 4 times b. 2 out of 4 times c. 3 out of 4 times d. 4 out of 4 times e. __% of the time f. in/for 0–5 seconds g. in/for 5–30 seconds h. in/for 30–60 seconds i. in/for over 1 minute j. in/for __ minutes k. 1 repetition l. 2–5 repetitions m. 6–10 repetitions n. over 10 repetitions o. __ repetitions p. 0–5 feet q. 5–15 feet r. 15–25 feet s. over 25 feet t. __ feet u. to/at mid range/level v. to/at functional range/level w. to/at normal limits x. to/at __% of normal y. to/at __ degrees

Increase of Muscle Strength and Endurance to within Normal Limits continued

Behaviors	Conditions	Measurements
73. develop the strength to perform functional activities on the playground 74. develop the endurance to perform functional activities in the classroom 75. develop the endurance to perform functional activities on the playground	A. with maximum– moderate assistance B. with moderate– minimum assistance C. with __% assistance D. with guarding assistance E. with facilitation F. with tactile cues G. with proprioceptive cues H. with a demonstration I. with verbal cues J. in the therapy setting K. independently L. in functional activities	a. 1 out of 4 times b. 2 out of 4 times c. 3 out of 4 times d. 4 out of 4 times e. __% of the time f. in/for 0–5 seconds g. in/for 5–30 seconds h. in/for 30–60 seconds i. in/for over 1 minute j. in/for __ minutes k. 1 repetition l. 2–5 repetitions m. 6–10 repetitions n. over 10 repetitions o. __ repetitions p. 0–5 feet q. 5–15 feet r. 15–25 feet s. over 25 feet t. __ feet u. to/at mid range/level v. to/at functional range/level w. to/at normal limits x. to/at __% of normal y. to/at __ degrees

Increased Range and Strength of Muscles Affecting Cardiopulmonary and Excretory Systems

Behaviors	Conditions	Measurements
The student will		
76. improve strength and effectiveness of cough	A. with maximum–moderate assistance	a. 1 out of 4 times
	B. with moderate–minimum assistance	b. 2 out of 4 times
77. increase thoracic mobility		c. 3 out of 4 times
78. increase cardiopulmonary capacity	C. with __% assistance	d. 4 out of 4 times
79. increase depth and decrease speed of respirations	D. with guarding assistance	e. __% of the time
	E. with facilitation	f. in/for 0–5 seconds
		g. in/for 5–30 seconds
80. dissociate chest expansions from trunk movement	F. with tactile cues	h. in/for 30–60 seconds
	G. with proprioceptive cues	i. in/for over 1 minute
81. maintain breathing rhythm during therapeutic activities	H. with a demonstration	j. in/for __ minutes
	I. with verbal cues	k. 1 repetition
82. maintain contraction of sphincter to delay bowel movement until sitting on the toilet	J. in the therapy setting	l. 2–5 repetitions
	K. independently	m. 6–10 repetitions
	L. in functional activities	n. over 10 repetitions
83. maintain contraction of sphincter to delay urinating until sitting on the toilet		o. __ repetitions
		p. 0–5 feet
		q. 5–15 feet
84. relax sphincter to move bowels when on the toilet		r. 15–25 feet
		s. over 25 feet
		t. __ feet
85. relax sphincter to urinate when on/at the toilet		u. to/at mid range/level
		v. to/at functional range/level
		w. to/at normal limits
		x. to/at __% of normal
		y. to/at __ degrees

Additional Objectives

Behaviors	Conditions	Measurements
The student will 86.	A. with maximum–moderate assistance B. with moderate–minimum assistance C. with __% assistance D. with guarding assistance E. with facilitation F. with tactile cues G. with proprioceptive cues H. with a demonstration I. with verbal cues J. in the therapy setting K. independently L. in functional activities	a. 1 out of 4 times b. 2 out of 4 times c. 3 out of 4 times d. 4 out of 4 times e. __% of the time f. in/for 0–5 seconds g. in/for 5–30 seconds h. in/for 30–60 seconds i. in/for over 1 minute j. in/for __ minutes k. 1 repetition l. 2–5 repetitions m. 6–10 repetitions n. over 10 repetitions o. __ repetitions p. 0–5 feet q. 5–15 feet r. 15–25 feet s. over 25 feet t. __ feet u. to/at mid range/level v. to/at functional range/level w. to/at normal limits x. to/at __% of normal y. to/at __ degrees

Gross Motor Planning VII

The many skills performed on the playground or in physical education are often a major concern of teachers, parents, children, and therapists. Some may not care how these skills are performed, but primarily want participation. Keeping a child off the playground for several years in order to refine early skills is not a reasonable solution. The child should be doing whatever possible to join his or her friends. But the child will fit in better, look better, and perform better in the long run if normal components and quality are addressed in therapy. If the child kneels and walks with a hyperextension posture, the hyperextension in running will be even worse. How effectively will the child ever be able to throw, jump, hop, or kick unless the therapist goes back and develops proximal stability and equilibrium in sitting, kneeling, and standing? Evaluation should not just determine if the child can hop, but whether he or she can hop on either foot, in the desired direction, with control, speed, and balance, and with dissociation of head and arms.

Planning and Executing Age Appropriate Gross Motor Skills Using Normal Movement Patterns

Behaviors	Conditions	Measurements
The student will 1. perform a sit-up with chin tucked 2. assume a position of supine flexion 3. maintain a position of supine flexion 4. maintain supine flexion with stability 5. maintain flexion while performing a somersault 6. maintain flexion while performing a backward somersault 7. display ____ degrees of elbow flexion while hanging from a horizontal bar 8. display ____ degrees of hip flexion while hanging from a horizontal bar 9. display over 90% of elbow, hip, and knee flexion while hanging from a horizontal bar 10. perform a push-up with pelvis in neutral 11. perform bridging with chin tucked 12. assume a position of prone extension 13. maintain a position of prone extension 14. maintain prone extension with stability 15. imitate an upper body static posture	A. with maximum– moderate assistance B. with moderate– minimum assistance C. with ___% assistance D. with guarding assistance E. with facilitation F. with tactile cues G. with proprioceptive cues H. with a demonstration I. with verbal cues J. in the therapy setting K. independently L. in functional activities	a. 1 out of 4 times b. 2 out of 4 times c. 3 out of 4 times d. 4 out of 4 times e. ___% of the time f. in/for 0–5 seconds g. in/for 5–30 seconds h. in/for 30–60 seconds i. in/for over 1 minute j. in/for ___ minutes k. 1 repetition l. 2–5 repetitions m. 6–10 repetitions n. over 10 repetitions o. ___ repetitions p. 0–5 feet q. 5–15 feet r. 15–25 feet s. over 25 feet t. ___ feet u. to/at mid range/level v. to/at functional range/level w. to/at normal limits x. to/at ___% of normal y. to/at ___ degrees

Planning and Executing Age Appropriate Gross Motor Skills Using Normal Movement Patterns continued

Behaviors	Conditions	Measurements
16. imitate a lower body static posture	A. with maximum–moderate assistance	a. 1 out of 4 times
17. imitate a whole body static posture		b. 2 out of 4 times
18. imitate a _____ step (2, 3, 4, 5) upper body motor pattern	B. with moderate–minimum assistance	c. 3 out of 4 times
	C. with _% assistance	d. 4 out of 4 times
19. imitate a _____ step (2, 3, 4, 5) lower body motor pattern	D. with guarding assistance	e. _% of the time
		f. in/for 0–5 seconds
20. imitate a _____ step (2, 3, 4, 5) whole body motor pattern	E. with facilitation	g. in/for 5–30 seconds
	F. with tactile cues	h. in/for 30–60 seconds
	G. with proprioceptive cues	i. in/for over 1 minute
21. catch a large ball with 2 hands		j. in/for _ minutes
22. catch a small ball with 2 hands	H. with a demonstration	k. 1 repetition
23. catch a small ball with 1 hand	I. with verbal cues	l. 2–5 repetitions
24. catch a ball with graded control	J. in the therapy setting	m. 6–10 repetitions
25. catch a ball while running	K. independently	n. over 10 repetitions
26. throw a large ball with 2 hands	L. in functional activities	o. _ repetitions
27. throw a ball at a target with 2 hands		p. 0–5 feet
28. throw a small ball with 1 hand		q. 5–15 feet
29. throw a ball at a target with 1 hand		r. 15–25 feet
30. throw a ball overhand		s. over 25 feet
31. throw with accuracy and graded control		t. _ feet
32. bounce a large ball with 2 hands		u. to/at mid range/level
33. bounce a large ball with 1 hand		v. to/at functional range/level
		w. to/at normal limits
		x. to/at _% of normal
		y. to/at _ degrees

Planning and Executing Age Appropriate Gross Motor Skills Using Normal Movement Patterns continued

Behaviors	Conditions	Measurements
34. bounce a large ball with the nondominant hand 35. bounce a small ball with 1 hand 36. bounce a small ball with the nondominant hand 37. bounce a ball with graded control 38. kick a large ball 39. kick a small ball 40. kick without hyperextension of head and arms 41. kick with weight forward 42. kick with graded control 43. kick a ball while running 44. log roll 45. roll in a straight line 46. roll segmentally 47. roll segmentally in a straight line 48. roll with graded control 49. wheelbarrow walk without lumbar lordosis 50. maintain balance while stooping to pick up an object	A. with maximum–moderate assistance B. with moderate–minimum assistance C. with __% assistance D. with guarding assistance E. with facilitation F. with tactile cues G. with proprioceptive cues H. with a demonstration I. with verbal cues J. in the therapy setting K. independently L. in functional activities	a. 1 out of 4 times b. 2 out of 4 times c. 3 out of 4 times d. 4 out of 4 times e. __% of the time f. in/for 0–5 seconds g. in/for 5–30 seconds h. in/for 30–60 seconds i. in/for over 1 minute j. in/for __ minutes k. 1 repetition l. 2–5 repetitions m. 6–10 repetitions n. over 10 repetitions o. __ repetitions p. 0–5 feet q. 5–15 feet r. 15–25 feet s. over 25 feet t. __ feet u. to/at mid range/level v. to/at functional range/level w. to/at normal limits x. to/at __% of normal y. to/at __ degrees

Planning and Executing Age Appropriate Gross Motor Skills Using Normal Movement Patterns continued

Behaviors	Conditions	Measurements
51. maintain balance in squatting	A. with maximum–moderate assistance	a. 1 out of 4 times
52. maintain balance in squatting during dynamic activities	B. with moderate–minimum assistance	b. 2 out of 4 times
53. assume a bear position	C. with __% assistance	c. 3 out of 4 times
54. maintain balance while bear walking	D. with guarding assistance	d. 4 out of 4 times
55. assume a crab position	E. with facilitation	e. __% of the time
56. maintain balance while crab walking	F. with tactile cues	f. in/for 0–5 seconds
57. maintain balance on an unstable surface	G. with proprioceptive cues	g. in/for 5–30 seconds
58. maintain balance while performing dynamic activities	H. with a demonstration	h. in/for 30–60 seconds
59. maintain balance while performing dynamic activities on an unstable surface	I. with verbal cues	i. in/for over 1 minute
60. walk sideways	J. in the therapy setting	j. in/for __ minutes
61. walk backward	K. independently	k. 1 repetition
62. walk on a straight line	L. in functional activities	l. 2–5 repetitions
63. walk on a curved line		m. 6–10 repetitions
64. walk backward on a straight line		n. over 10 repetitions
65. walk heel-to-toe on a straight line		o. __ repetitions
66. walk backward heel-to-toe on a straight line		p. 0–5 feet
67. walk on a straight line without excessive arm movements		q. 5–15 feet
		r. 15–25 feet
		s. over 25 feet
		t. __ feet
		u. to/at mid range/level
		v. to/at functional range/level
		w. to/at normal limits
		x. to/at __% of normal
		y. to/at __ degrees

Planning and Executing Age Appropriate Gross Motor Skills Using Normal Movement Patterns continued

Behaviors	*Conditions*	*Measurements*
68. walk on a straight line with graded control	A. with maximum–moderate assistance	a. 1 out of 4 times
69. stand on a balance beam	B. with moderate–minimum assistance	b. 2 out of 4 times
70. walk forward on a balance beam	C. with __% assistance	c. 3 out of 4 times
71. walk backward on a balance beam	D. with guarding assistance	d. 4 out of 4 times
72. walk heel-to-toe on a balance beam	E. with facilitation	e. __% of the time
73. walk backward heel-to-toe on a balance beam	F. with tactile cues	f. in/for 0–5 seconds
74. walk on a balance beam without excessive arm movements	G. with proprioceptive cues	g. in/for 5–30 seconds
75. walk on a balance beam with graded control	H. with a demonstration	h. in/for 30–60 seconds
76. walk between rungs of a horizontal ladder without touching them	I. with verbal cues	i. in/for over 1 minute
77. maneuver through an obstacle course	J. in the therapy setting	j. in/for __ minutes
78. walk on tiptoe without hyperextension posturing	K. independently	k. 1 repetition
79. heel walk	L. in functional activities	l. 2–5 repetitions
80. run forward		m. 6–10 repetitions
81. run backward		n. over 10 repetitions
82. run without hyperextension posturing		o. __ repetitions
83. run with weight forward and arms pumping		p. 0–5 feet
		q. 5–15 feet
		r. 15–25 feet
		s. over 25 feet
		t. __ feet
		u. to/at mid range/level
		v. to/at functional range/level
		w. to/at normal limits
		x. to/at __% of normal
		y. to/at __ degrees

Planning and Executing Age Appropriate Gross Motor Skills Using Normal Movement Patterns continued

Behaviors	Conditions	Measurements
84. run with graded control	A. with maximum–moderate assistance	a. 1 out of 4 times
85. run through an obstacle course		b. 2 out of 4 times
86. stop quickly from a run	B. with moderate–minimum assistance	c. 3 out of 4 times
87. jump with upper extremity support	C. with __% assistance	d. 4 out of 4 times
88. jump	D. with guarding assistance	e. __% of the time
89. jump without hyperextension posturing	E. with facilitation	f. in/for 0–5 seconds
90. jump with both feet pushing off together	F. with tactile cues	g. in/for 5–30 seconds
91. jump down from a step	G. with proprioceptive cues	h. in/for 30–60 seconds
92. jump forward	H. with a demonstration	i. in/for over 1 minute
93. jump forward on a straight line	I. with verbal cues	j. in/for __ minutes
94. broad jump	J. in the therapy setting	k. 1 repetition
95. jump up in the air	K. independently	l. 2–5 repetitions
96. jump over a barrier	L. in functional activities	m. 6–10 repetitions
97. jump backward		n. over 10 repetitions
98. jump backward on a straight line		o. __ repetitions
99. jump up and down in one spot		p. 0–5 feet
100. maintain balance standing on one foot		q. 5–15 feet
101. stand on one foot with arms crossed on chest with control		r. 15–25 feet
102. maintain standing on one foot with eyes closed		s. over 25 feet
		t. __ feet
		u. to/at mid range/level
		v. to/at functional range/level
		w. to/at normal limits
		x. to/at __% of normal
		y. to/at __ degrees

Planning and Executing Age Appropriate Gross Motor Skills Using Normal Movement Patterns continued

Behaviors	Conditions	Measurements
103. stand on one foot with arms crossed on chest and eyes closed with control	A. with maximum–moderate assistance	a. 1 out of 4 times
104. hop on the dominant side	B. with moderate–minimum assistance	b. 2 out of 4 times
105. hop on the dominant side without hyperextension posturing	C. with __% assistance	c. 3 out of 4 times
106. hop on the nondominant side	D. with guarding assistance	d. 4 out of 4 times
107. hop on the nondominant side without hyperextension posturing	E. with facilitation	e. __% of the time
108. hop forward on a straight line	F. with tactile cues	f. in/for 0–5 seconds
109. hop on alternate sides	G. with proprioceptive cues	g. in/for 5–30 seconds
110. imitate a _____ step (2, 3, 4, 5) hop-jump pattern	H. with a demonstration	h. in/for 30–60 seconds
111. perform a jumping jack	I. with verbal cues	i. in/for over 1 minute
112. jump rope forward	J. in the therapy setting	j. in/for __ minutes
113. jump rope backward	K. independently	k. 1 repetition
114. march	L. in functional activities	l. 2–5 repetitions
115. gallop		m. 6–10 repetitions
116. gallop with alternating foot leads		n. over 10 repetitions
117. gallop with graded control		o. __ repetitions
118. half-skip		p. 0–5 feet
119. skip		q. 5–15 feet
		r. 15–25 feet
		s. over 25 feet
		t. __ feet
		u. to/at mid range/level
		v. to/at functional range/level
		w. to/at normal limits
		x. to/at __% of normal
		y. to/at __ degrees

Planning and Executing Age Appropriate Gross Motor Skills Using Normal Movement Patterns continued

Behaviors	Conditions	Measurements
120. skip without excessive movement of arms 121. skip symmetrically and smoothly 122. keep weight forward in gross motor activities 123. perform gross motor activities without hyperextension posturing 124. prevent trunk collapse in gross motor activities 125. demonstrate the components of equilibrium in gross motor activities 126. perform gross motor activities with graded control 127. ride a tricycle 128. ride a bicycle 129. use/climb on playground equipment 130. demonstrate sufficient balance and control for unsupervised use of playground equipment	A. with maximum–moderate assistance B. with moderate–minimum assistance C. with __% assistance D. with guarding assistance E. with facilitation F. with tactile cues G. with proprioceptive cues H. with a demonstration I. with verbal cues J. in the therapy setting K. independently L. in functional activities	a. 1 out of 4 times b. 2 out of 4 times c. 3 out of 4 times d. 4 out of 4 times e. __% of the time f. in/for 0–5 seconds g. in/for 5–30 seconds h. in/for 30–60 seconds i. in/for over 1 minute j. in/for __ minutes k. 1 repetition l. 2–5 repetitions m. 6–10 repetitions n. over 10 repetitions o. __ repetitions p. 0–5 feet q. 5–15 feet r. 15–25 feet s. over 25 feet t. __ feet u. to/at mid range/level v. to/at functional range/level w. to/at normal limits x. to/at __% of normal y. to/at __ degrees

Additional Objectives

Behaviors	Conditions	Measurements
The student will 131.	A. with maximum–moderate assistance B. with moderate–minimum assistance C. with __% assistance D. with guarding assistance E. with facilitation F. with tactile cues G. with proprioceptive cues H. with a demonstration I. with verbal cues J. in the therapy setting K. independently L. in functional activities	a. 1 out of 4 times b. 2 out of 4 times c. 3 out of 4 times d. 4 out of 4 times e. __% of the time f. in/for 0–5 seconds g. in/for 5–30 seconds h. in/for 30–60 seconds i. in/for over 1 minute j. in/for __ minutes k. 1 repetition l. 2–5 repetitions m. 6–10 repetitions n. over 10 repetitions o. __ repetitions p. 0–5 feet q. 5–15 feet r. 15–25 feet s. over 25 feet t. __ feet u. to/at mid range/level v. to/at functional range/level w. to/at normal limits x. to/at __% of normal y. to/at __ degrees

Psychosensory Effects on Therapy   VIII

Although this manual deals with gross motor development, no therapy program exists that is not influenced by behavior, attitude, and response to sensory input. The objectives in this section relate to these factors as they affect a therapy program of gross motor goals. Frequently children starting therapy can be worked with only after weeks of accustoming them to handling and encouraging their cooperation and acceptance of certain pieces of equipment. A child for whom the therapist's main goal is to develop equilibrium in sitting may require initial objectives such as "tolerate handling," "cooperate for length of treatment session," etc. A responsible, motivated student with the same motor deficits could work on different behavioral objectives, possibly including "take responsibility for using correct movement patterns."

Increased Tolerance and Awareness of Sensory Input for the Performance of Appropriate Therapeutic Activities

Behaviors	Conditions	Measurements
The student will 1. maintain physical control with unexpected tactile stimuli 2. demonstrate reduced aversion to tactile stimuli 3. tolerate firm touch 4. tolerate light, moving touch 5. show awareness of tactile stimuli 6. show a specific response to tactile stimuli 7. tolerate linear movement 8. tolerate vertical movement 9. tolerate rotatory movement 10. tolerate movement controlled by the student 11. tolerate movement controlled by the therapist 12. tolerate positioning on stable equipment 13. tolerate positioning on moving equipment 14. tolerate positioning with feet higher than head	A. with maximum–moderate assistance B. with moderate–minimum assistance C. with __% assistance D. with guarding assistance E. with facilitation F. with tactile cues G. with proprioceptive cues H. with a demonstration I. with verbal cues J. in the therapy setting K. independently L. in functional activities	a. 1 out of 4 times b. 2 out of 4 times c. 3 out of 4 times d. 4 out of 4 times e. __% of the time f. in/for 0–5 seconds g. in/for 5–30 seconds h. in/for 30–60 seconds i. in/for over 1 minute j. in/for __ minutes k. 1 repetition l. 2–5 repetitions m. 6–10 repetitions n. over 10 repetitions o. __ repetitions p. 0–5 feet q. 5–15 feet r. 15–25 feet s. over 25 feet t. __ feet u. to/at mid range/level v. to/at functional range/level w. to/at normal limits x. to/at __% of normal y. to/at __ degrees

Increased Tolerance and Awareness of Sensory Input for the Performance of Appropriate Therapeutic Activities continued

Behaviors	Conditions	Measurements
15. tolerate an upside-down position 16. jump off the floor 17. climb on stable equipment 18. climb on moving equipment 19. tolerate joint compression 20. respond to joint compression with antigravity stabilization 21. respond to manual resistance with a contraction of the opposed muscle or muscle groups 22. identify major body parts 23. distinguish left from right sides of body 24. show awareness of the hemiparetic side 25. use the hemiparetic side 26. use the hemiparetic upper extremity as an assist 27. use the hemiparetic upper extremity in bilateral activities 28. recognize need to move bowels 29. recognize need to urinate	A. with maximum–moderate assistance B. with moderate–minimum assistance C. with __% assistance D. with guarding assistance E. with facilitation F. with tactile cues G. with proprioceptive cues H. with a demonstration I. with verbal cues J. in the therapy setting K. independently L. in functional activities	a. 1 out of 4 times b. 2 out of 4 times c. 3 out of 4 times d. 4 out of 4 times e. __% of the time f. in/for 0–5 seconds g. in/for 5–30 seconds h. in/for 30–60 seconds i. in/for over 1 minute j. in/for __ minutes k. 1 repetition l. 2–5 repetitions m. 6–10 repetitions n. over 10 repetitions o. __ repetitions p. 0–5 feet q. 5–15 feet r. 15–25 feet s. over 25 feet t. __ feet u. to/at mid range/level v. to/at functional range/level w. to/at normal limits x. to/at __% of normal y. to/at __ degrees

Development of Self-Motivation in Performing Therapeutic Activities

Behaviors	Conditions	Measurements
The student will	A with maximum–moderate assistance	a. 1 out of 4 times
30. tolerate handling	B. with moderate–minimum assistance	b. 2 out of 4 times
31. cooperate in active exercises	C. with ___% assistance	c. 3 out of 4 times
32. cooperate for length of treatment session	D. with guarding assistance	d. 4 out of 4 times
33. follow safety guidelines in independent ambulation	E. with facilitation	e. ___% of the time
34. follow safety guidelines in wheelchair use	F. with tactile cues	f. in/for 0–5 seconds
35. take responsibility for using adaptive equipment appropriately	G. with proprioceptive cues	g. in/for 5–30 seconds
36. take responsibility for maintaining the proper sitting posture in classroom activities	H. with a demonstration	h. in/for 30–60 seconds
37. take responsibility for using correct movement patterns	I. with verbal cues	i. in/for over 1 minute
38. take responsibility for performing ADL as independently as possible	J. in the therapy setting	j. in/for ___ minutes
39. take responsibility for allowing sufficient time to get to a toilet	K. independently	k. 1 repetition
40. take responsibility for carrying out a recommended home exercise program	L. in functional activities	l. 2–5 repetitions

The student will

30. tolerate handling

31. cooperate in active exercises

32. cooperate for length of treatment session

33. follow safety guidelines in independent ambulation

34. follow safety guidelines in wheelchair use

35. take responsibility for using adaptive equipment appropriately

36. take responsibility for maintaining the proper sitting posture in classroom activities

37. take responsibility for using correct movement patterns

38. take responsibility for performing ADL as independently as possible

39. take responsibility for allowing sufficient time to get to a toilet

40. take responsibility for carrying out a recommended home exercise program

Conditions

A with maximum–moderate assistance
B. with moderate–minimum assistance
C. with ___% assistance
D. with guarding assistance
E. with facilitation
F. with tactile cues
G. with proprioceptive cues
H. with a demonstration
I. with verbal cues
J. in the therapy setting
K. independently
L. in functional activities

Measurements

a. 1 out of 4 times
b. 2 out of 4 times
c. 3 out of 4 times
d. 4 out of 4 times
e. ___% of the time
f. in/for 0–5 seconds
g. in/for 5–30 seconds
h. in/for 30–60 seconds
i. in/for over 1 minute
j. in/for ___ minutes
k. 1 repetition
l. 2–5 repetitions
m. 6–10 repetitions
n. over 10 repetitions
o. ___ repetitions
p. 0–5 feet
q. 5–15 feet
r. 15–25 feet
s. over 25 feet
t. ___ feet
u. to/at mid range/level
v. to/at functional range/level
w. to/at normal limits
x. to/at ___% of normal
y. to/at ___ degrees

Additional Objectives

Behaviors	Conditions	Measurements
The student will 41.	A. with maximum–moderate assistance B. with moderate–minimum assistance C. with __% assistance D. with guarding assistance E. with facilitation F. with tactile cues G. with proprioceptive cues H. with a demonstration I. with verbal cues J. in the therapy setting K. independently L. in functional activities	a. 1 out of 4 times b. 2 out of 4 times c. 3 out of 4 times d. 4 out of 4 times e. __% of the time f. in/for 0–5 seconds g. in/for 5–30 seconds h. in/for 30–60 seconds i. in/for over 1 minute j. in/for __ minutes k. 1 repetition l. 2–5 repetitions m. 6–10 repetitions n. over 10 repetitions o. __ repetitions p. 0–5 feet q. 5–15 feet r. 15–25 feet s. over 25 feet t. __ feet u. to/at mid range/level v. to/at functional range/level w. to/at normal limits x. to/at __% of normal y. to/at __ degrees

Activities of Daily Living   Appendix

Numbers refer to sections and behaviors. For example, I-27 refers to behavior 27 in Section I.

ADL (nonspecific)

I-27 Inhibit flailing while being assisted in ADL
I-28 Maintain relaxation while being assisted in ADL
I-111 Maintain reduced tonus in an upright posture for ADL
II-76 Shift weight for ADL
III-208 Maintain stability in sitting for ADL
IV-147 Use upper extremity prostheses in ADL
VI-23 Increase range of shoulder girdle to allow sufficient mobility for ADL
VIII-38 Take responsibility for performing ADL as independently as possible

Bathing

I-26 Maintain relaxation while being bathed
II-79 Use equilibrium reactions to maintain sitting balance in bathtub
II-82 Maintain balance while stepping into bathtub
II-83 Maintain balance during transitions between sitting and standing in bathtub
III-124 Stabilize shoulder girdle to wash body while sitting in a chair

III-125 Stabilize shoulder girdle to wash body while sitting in a bathtub
III-198 Maintain stability seated in a bathtub
III-310 Step into bathtub
III-311 Grade transitions between sitting and standing in a bathtub
V-34 Perform transfers between the wheelchair and a bathtub

Dressing

I-22 Maintain relaxation while being diapered
I-24 Maintain relaxation while being dressed
I-69 Bring head/trunk forward to help in dressing
I-70 Raise arm(s) to help in dressing
I-71 Raise leg(s) to help in dressing
I-72 Bring hands together to help in dressing
I-86 Perform bridging to assist in dressing
II-77 Use equilibrium reactions to maintain sitting balance during dressing
II-81 Use equilibrium reactions to maintain standing balance during dressing

III-99 Stabilize shoulder girdle to adjust clothing in preparation for toiletting

III-100 Stabilize shoulder girdle to adjust clothing following toiletting

III-126 Stabilize shoulder girdle for self-dressing

III-127 Dissociate body parts for dressing activities

III-128 Bring hands together for dressing activities

III-129 Hold arm out for dressing

III-130 Hold leg/foot out for dressing

III-131 Push arms through sleeves

III-132 Push legs through pants

III-133 Stabilize shoulder girdle to remove hat

III-134 Stabilize shoulder girdle to put on hat

III-135 Stabilize shoulder girdle to remove shoes and socks

III-136 Stabilize shoulder girdle to push bottom garment down past buttocks

III-137 Stabilize shoulder girdle to remove coat

III-138 Stabilize shoulder girdle to remove tops with front opening

III-139 Stabilize shoulder girdle to remove pants

III-140 Stabilize shoulder girdle to remove tops over the head

III-141 Stabilize shoulder girdle to remove underclothing

III-142 Stabilize shoulder girdle to put on tops over the head

III-143 Stabilize shoulder girdle to put on coat

III-144 Stabilize shoulder girdle to put on tops with front opening

III-145 Stabilize shoulder girdle to put on underclothing

III-146 Stabilize shoulder girdle to put on pants

III-147 Stabilize shoulder girdle to put on shoes

III-148 Stabilize shoulder girdle to put on socks

III-149 Stabilize shoulder girdle to undo fastenings

III-150 Stabilize shoulder girdle to undo a _____ type fastening

III-151 Stabilize shoulder girdle to undo fastenings on own clothing

III-152 Stabilize shoulder girdle to undo a _____ type fastening on own clothing

III-153 Stabilize shoulder girdle to do up fastenings

III-154 Stabilize shoulder girdle to do up a _____ type fastening

III-155 Stabilize shoulder girdle to do up fastenings on own clothing

III-156 Stabilize shoulder girdle to do up a _____ type fastening on own clothing

III-157 Stabilize shoulder girdle to tie shoes

III-309 Stand on one foot for dressing activities

IV-149 Put on and take off upper extremity prostheses

IV-151 Put on and take off upper extremity splints

IV-162 Remove braces or prostheses

IV-163 Put on braces or prostheses

V-26 Adjust clothing in wheelchair in order to use a urinal

V-28 Adjust clothing in wheelchair in order to use a toilet

Feeding

I-150 Suck from a bottle

I-151 Maintain head in neutral to accept food

I-152 Remove food from spoon with top lip closure

I-153 Maintain head in neutral to drink

I-154 Seal lips on cup to drink

I-155 Bite food

I-156 Maintain head in neutral to bite food

I-157 Chew food

I-158 Maintain head in neutral to chew food

I-159 Keep food in mouth while chewing

I-160 Swallow easy textures of food (puréed, mashed, springy) without choking

I-161 Swallow difficult textures of food (slippery, crumbly, sticky) without choking

I-162 Swallow liquids without choking

I-163 Finger feed self

I-164 Maintain head in neutral to finger feed

I-165 Feed self with spoon

I-166 Maintain head in neutral to feed self with spoon

III-104 Stabilize shoulder girdle for self-feeding

III-105 Stabilize shoulder girdle to finger feed self

III-106 Stabilize shoulder girdle to feed self with spoon with spilling

III-107 Stabilize shoulder girdle to feed self with spoon without spilling

III-108 Stabilize shoulder girdle to feed self with adaptive spoon

III-109 Stabilize shoulder girdle to scoop with spoon

III-110 Stabilize shoulder girdle to bring cup to mouth with spilling

III-111 Stabilize shoulder girdle to bring cup to mouth without spilling

Toiletting

I-22 Maintain relaxation while being diapered

I-23 Maintain relaxation while being toiletted

II-78 Use equilibrium reactions to maintain sitting balance on toilet

III-95 Stabilize shoulder girdle for support in toiletting

III-96 Stabilize shoulder girdle to hold front support bar during toiletting

III-97 Stabilize shoulder girdle to reach for and hold grab bars during toiletting

III-98 Stabilize shoulder girdle to reach behind to hold grab bars during toiletting

III-99 Stabilize shoulder girdle to adjust clothing in preparation for toiletting

III-100 Stabilize shoulder girdle to adjust clothing following toiletting

III-101 Stabilize shoulder girdle to wipe self from front after using toilet

III-102 Stabilize shoulder girdle to wipe self from back after using toilet

III-103 Stabilize shoulder girdle to put on and remove sanitary pads

III-136 Stabilize shoulder girdle to push bottom garment down past buttocks

III-196 Maintain stability seated on an adaptive toilet

III-197 Maintain stability seated on a toilet

V-25 Perform transfers between the wheelchair and a standing position at a urinal

V-26 Adjust clothing in wheelchair in order to use a urinal

V-27 Perform transfers between the wheelchair and a toilet

V-28 Adjust clothing in wheelchair in order to use a toilet

VI-82 Maintain contraction of sphincter to delay bowel movement until sitting on the toilet

VI-83 Maintain contraction of sphincter to delay urinating until sitting on a toilet

VI-84 Relax sphincter to move bowels when on the toilet

VI-85 Relax sphincter to urinate when on/at the toilet

VIII-28 Recognize need to move bowels

VIII-29 Recognize need to urinate

VIII-39 Take responsibility for allowing sufficient time to get to a toilet

Washing and Grooming

I-25 Maintain relaxation during washing and grooming

I-126 Allow tooth brushing

III-103 Stabilize shoulder girdle to put on and remove sanitary pads

III-112 Stabilize shoulder girdle for grooming activities

III-113 Stabilize shoulder girdle to hold and raise toothbrush to mouth

III-114 Stabilize shoulder girdle to put toothpaste on a toothbrush

III-115 Stabilize shoulder girdle to use a toothbrush

III-116 Stabilize shoulder girdle to wash hands

III-117 Stabilize shoulder girdle to dry hands

III-118 Stabilize shoulder girdle to hold a washcloth

III-119 Stabilize shoulder girdle to wash face with a washcloth

III-120 Stabilize shoulder girdle to turn a faucet on and off

III-121 Stabilize proximal joints to hold a comb or brush

III-122 Stabilize shoulder girdle to raise arm to back of head for combing or brushing

III-123 Stabilize shoulder girdle to comb or brush hair

III-124 Stabilize shoulder girdle to wash body while sitting in a chair

Index of Behaviors

Numbers refer to sections and behaviors. For example, IV-53–55 refers to behaviors 53 to 55 in Section IV.